A MATTER OF
LIFE
AND
DEATH

A MATTER OF
LIFE
AND
DEATH

JAMES L. HOLLY, M.D.

FOREWORD BY JOHN F. MacARTHUR, JR.

BROADMAN
&HOLMAN
PUBLISHERS

Nashville, Tennessee

0-8054-6282-1

Dewey Decimal Classification: 241.69
Subject heading: Pro-Life Movement Violence \ Sanctity of Life
Library of Congress Card Catalog Number: 95-16513

All Scripture quotations, unless otherwise noted, are from the King
James Version. Those marked AMP are from The Amplified Bible, copyright © 1987 by the Zondervan Corporation and The Lockman
Foundation, and are used by permission. Those marked NASB are from
the New American Standard Bible, © 1960, 1962, 1963, 1968, 1971,
1972, 1973, 1975, and 1977 by The Lockman Foundation, and are
used by permission. Those marked PHILLIPS are from The New
Testament in Modern English by J. B. Phillips, published by the
Macmillan Company, © 1958, 1960, 1972 by J. B. Phillips. Those
marked TLB are from The Living Bible, copyright © 1971, Tyndale
House Publishers, Wheaton, Ill., and are used by permission.

Library of Congress Cataloging-in-Publication-Data
Holly, James L.
    A matter of life and death : what the Bible has to say about
violence in the pro-life movement / James L. Holly.
        p. cm.
    Includes bibliographical references.
    ISBN 0-8054-6282-1
    1. Abortion—Religious aspects—Christianity.   2. Pro-Life move-
ment—Religious aspects—Christianity.   3. Violence—Religious aspects
—Christianity.   I. Title.
    HQ767.25.H65   1995
    291.5'6976—dc20   95-16513
                                                        CIP

To Joey

PUBLISHER'S NOTE

Dr. James L. Holly has written a provocative book that calls Christians to consider their course of action in fighting abortion. The book will stimulate your thinking and challenge you to respond to these issues. Dr. Holly persuasively argues his position and presents his prescriptions. While we too deplore violence, not all of his arguments and recommendations are necessarily those of the publisher. In making this book available, it is our prayer that Christians will pay particular attention to the issues involved and, that consistent with the word of God and with the character of Jesus Christ, they will engage the battle as they are led by the Holy Spirit.

Charles A. Wilson
Publisher
Broadman & Holman

Contents

FOREWORD

WHEN SELF-STYLED "PRO-LIFE" advocates began killing abortion providers, both friends and foes of the anti-abortion crusade wondered aloud whether a movement that breeds such atrocities has any right to label itself "pro-life." The problem was only worsened when some anti-abortion groups could not seem to muster sincere outrage over the killings.

Most grass-roots Christians have been shocked and saddened by these events. When and where did the pro-life movement take so wrong a turn? How did the actions and rhetoric of an essentially noble movement become so fraught with fury, threats, violence—now even bloodshed?

Almost ten years ago, pro-life leaders began to solicit Christians to participate in various forms of public protest and political activism. Several groups advanced arguments in favor of civil disobedience—actually encouraging Christians to violate the law as a means of demonstration. Thousands dutifully followed that course. They purposely committed acts to get themselves arrested, believing they were doing the will of God.

Almost predictably, the very same arguments that were used to defend such actions have been hijacked by fanatics who are using them to justify brutal killings. Pro-life leaders who have goaded their own people into civil disobedience now find it difficult, if not impossible, to marshal the troops in opposition to the violence extremists. The pro-violent factions have become bolder and bolder. They have even produced clean-cut, articulate spokesmen who go on national television and openly advocate the bombing of clinics and the murder of abortionists. Talk shows and tabloids are in a feeding frenzy. Suddenly the spotlight reveals a surprisingly widespread sinister side of the crusade against abortion.

Dr. Larry Holly has watched these events unfold. Like many of us, he opposes abortion on biblical grounds. But he reminds us what the Savior told Peter when that impetuous disciple illegally wielded a weapon on that fateful night in the garden: "Put up again thy sword into his place: for all they that take the sword shall perish with the sword" (Matt. 26:52).

Dr. Holly gives a thorough history of violence in the pro-life movement. He chronicles the rise of civil disobedience and analyzes the rhetoric used to support illegal tactics. And he gives a carefully reasoned, biblical response. This book should be required reading for all Christians active in the pro-life movement.

While reading this valuable work I was constantly reminded that the battle against abortion is essentially a spiritual one. It cannot be fought with fleshly weapons. Violent and illegal acts only benefit the enemy. Public protests, sit-ins, demonstrations, and other forms of media exploitation cannot ultimately overturn the spiritual malaise that has made society tolerant of abortions. The only real answer is widespread spiritual regeneration—in earlier times known as revival.

Church history proves that when Christianity joins with a political movement, the church's testimony inevitably fails. Christian leaders—especially pastors—must remember that the pulpit cannot become a platform for political agitation. Partisan causes, however noble, must not dissuade the church from the high spiritual calling of our Lord's Great Commission. Evangelicals must not turn away from our true spiritual mission or be fooled into thinking that our greatest battles are in the arena of secular politics.

In other words, we cannot sacrifice the eternal for the sake of the temporal. We must not forfeit spiritual ground for the sake of political gain. Political victories are too short-lived. Even legislation outlawing abortion—as desirable as that is—is only a partial solution. The real problem underlying the rise of abortions is something deeper than merely moral decline. The deeper problem is that millions are hopelessly enslaved to sin, unregenerate, without Christ, without God, and without hope. Laws, while necessary to curtail the spread of evil, cannot make an ungodly society righteous. Alcoholism, crime, drugs, homosexuality, and other moral issues provide ample proof of that. Again, the only ultimate hope for victory is a widespread spiritual awakening in which millions become new creatures in Christ.

Before that awakening can happen, the church must regain a biblical perspective and return to godly means of ministry. Why should Christians mimic the world's strategies of demonstration, protest, and civil disobedience? There are so many better ways we can legitimately and positively make a difference in the struggle against abortion. Concerned Christians can help by providing emotional support and financial assistance for women faced with unwanted pregnancies. They can, for example, open their homes to unwed mothers, demonstrating Christ's love in action in the framework of a loving family environment. They can adopt unwanted children or work with organizations that help find Christian families who are willing to adopt. They can educate people in their sphere of influence about the evils of abortion and show how Scripture applies to the issue. They can work with and support evangelical-based crisis pregnancy centers and other ministries that assist women seeking alternatives to abortion. Above all, they can fearlessly proclaim the gospel of redemption in Jesus Christ.

Many Christians are already actively involved in these and similar efforts. Their work is making a real difference, even though their efforts are not highly publicized. All genuine followers of Christ need to unite in support of such efforts. We also must with one voice condemn illegal violence and renounce those who want us to employ carnal weapons in this intensely spiritual battle.

If you are pondering these issues, I can think of no better resource than the book you now hold in your hands. I appreciate Dr. Holly's thoroughness, his commitment to Scripture, his courage in speaking out, and his diligence in producing the best reply to pro-life extremism I have ever read. I commend it with great enthusiasm.

JOHN F. MACARTHUR JR.

Though we walk in the flesh, we do not war according to the flesh, for the weapons of our warfare are not of the flesh, but divinely powerful for the destruction of fortresses.

2 CORINTHIANS 10:3–4, NASB

PREFACE

ON MARCH 2, 1995, MICHAEL GRIFFIN, who is serving a life sentence for the murder of an abortionist, said, "I used to believe [the killing of an abortionist] was justifiable homicide. I don't anymore."[1] His repentance may give others pause before they undertake the same course of action. Ultimately, the only hope Christians have for stopping abortion in America is a strong, vibrant church that is Spirit-filled, Spirit-led, and true to God's inerrant, eternal, immutable, and universal Word. I pray that we will see revival sweep America, bringing a return to God's standards of holiness and righteousness.

It was inevitable that this book would be written; it was improbable that I would write it. Yet, after years of marching in and speaking at pro-life rallies, of practicing aggressive pro-life medicine—opposing abortion for anyone, at any time, for any reason—of publicly opposing the fatal assault on Dr. David Gunn, of privately dialoguing with Paul Hill and Father David Trosch, and of publicly debating Michael Bray, perhaps it was inevitable that I should write it.

This book is written with the same confession given before a group of university women to whom I spoke a number of years ago. I said to them, "Everything which I say to you tonight has to be understood in the context of an experience I had when I was seventeen years old. As a college freshman, I met a man who obviously knew God personally. I discovered that I was a sinner, lost, and on my way to hell. Jesus Christ saved my soul and gave me a purpose to live." A woman in that group turned to a young lady sitting next to her and said, "That's the most disgusting thing I have ever heard." Whereupon, the young person smiled and said loudly, "I know. That's my daddy!"

This book is offered to the body of Christ from the heart of a father, whose Heavenly Father has said of His Son, "This is my beloved Son, in whom I am well pleased; hear ye him" (Matt. 17:5). If we can hear the heart of the Father in the words of the Son, through the ministry of God, the Holy Spirit, no matter what happens with abortion in America, we can be righteous and the reign of Christ as Lord and King can be extended to our lives.

Acknowledgments of those who have made major contributions to this work are numerous, which itself suggests this work is a product of the body of Christ and not one individual. Many responded to a questionnaire about the issues in this book. I am grateful for each one. Walter Collett motivated this work by inviting me to debate these issues publicly. Russell Kaemmerling forced me to narrow my focus and served as a faithful critic throughout the writing of this book. Dr. Kurt Richardson suggested several fruitful areas of research. Mark Brooks, Tommy French, Terry Long, Brad Salyer, and Ray Reed contributed to the editing and critiquing of the manuscript in process.

Finally, no one deserves greater credit than my wife. Carolyn Holly has endured the years of my preaching the truth; she has stood by me and for me. She has counseled me and chided me. She has encouraged me and has edited my work. She perfectly epitomizes what God meant for a wife to be. She is also the grandmother of the most wonderful grandson and soon-to-be-born granddaughter that have ever walked the face of the earth. It is for the children that we battle against abortion and violence, both of which are a threat to their future.

To each of these, I give grateful thanksgiving that they have contributed to making this work better than it would have been without their input, without making them responsible for any deficiencies which remain.

In light of the April 19th bombing of the Federal Building in Oklahoma City, the principles in this book become doubly important. All of the issues raised in this book—the relationship between rhetoric and revolution, the responsibility of Christians to be righteous as well as right, and the rejection of force and/or violence as methods for advancing one's personal convictions—apply to the use of terrorism for the redress of imagined grievances against the government. It is my hope and prayer that this book will provoke a dialogue which will enable Christians to have a clear voice on the ethical and moral issues which face the church today.

> *Bow down thine ear, and hear the words of the wise, and apply thine heart unto my knowledge. For it is a pleasant thing if thou keep them within thee; they shall withal be fitted in thy lips. That thy trust may be in the LORD, I have made known to thee this day, even to thee. Have not I written to thee excellent things in counsels and knowledge, That I might make thee know the certainty of the words of truth; that thou mightest answer the words of truth to them that send unto thee?*
>
> PROVERBS 22:17–21

1

VIOLENCE THAT DEMANDS A RESPONSE

TWO SHOT-GUNNED TO DEATH"—so read newspaper headlines all over America on July 30, 1994. A slaying in Pensacola, Florida, had taken the lives of an abortionist and his escort. Violence against abortion clinics had reached new levels.

A Chronicle of Violence

Pensacola was the site of this move toward violence. On June 24, 1984, the Ladies' Center for Abortion was bombed. On Christmas Day 1984, the same clinic and the offices of two doctors who performed abortions were bombed. In March 1986, six anti-abortion protesters were arrested for injuring two women and damaging equipment at the Ladies' Center.

Americans are accustomed to headlines about the terrorism of the Irish Republican Army or Shiite Muslims, but they have been slow to respond to the growing level of nonpersonal, ideological violence in their own land. Anti-abortion violence increased radically in 1993.

- **February:** Abortion clinics were burned in Venice, Florida, and Corpus Christi, Texas.

1

- **March:** An abortion clinic in Missoula, Montana, was set on fire and destroyed. Michael Griffin shot and killed Dr. David Gunn outside a Pensacola abortion clinic. Instantly, the discussion of anti-abortion violence changed forever. The unthinkable had taken place: a human life had been taken in the name of saving human life. Surely, everyone thought, this is simply the random act of a deranged, emotionally unstable person.

- **May:** Abortion clinics were burned in Boise, Idaho, and Forest Grove, Oregon.

- **August:** The nonfatal shooting of abortionist Dr. George Tiller in Wichita, Kansas, raised new fears about a pattern as the violence continued.

- **September:** An abortion clinic was burned in Bakersfield, California.

- **October:** An abortion clinic in Houston, Texas, was burned as the pace of violent activities increased.

In 1988, nonviolent civil disobedience was begun by Operation Rescue, a nationwide organization founded by Randall Terry and based in Atlanta, Georgia. Operation Rescue prepared the way for the violent destruction of abortion clinics, which culminated in the logical conclusion of justifying illegal conduct, including the killing, not only of abortionists, but also of innocent companions. The unthinkable became reality. Pro-life and Christian leaders could no longer remain silent, tacitly approving and privately applauding that which they themselves would not do.

The First Murder
With the death of Dr. David Gunn in 1993, several previously unknown personalities came forward. Paul Hill

appeared on *The Phil Donahue Show, Nightline,* and other national television shows. He identified himself as having "pastored churches affiliated with the Presbyterian Church in America and the Orthodox Presbyterian Church." Excommunicated from his church when he refused to recant his pro-violence, anti-abortion stance, Hill began to publish his ideas on "defensive action." His tract, *Who Killed the Innocent—Michael Griffin or Dr. David Gunn?,* attempted to justify the killing of abortionists. He argued, "Defending the preborn with the same force with which we defend the born is not only just, it also demonstrates to the world that preborn humans are in fact humans. Consistent defensive action will cause men to decide between promoting the bloody death of unborn children and protecting innocent life."

Hill then circulated his statement entitled, *Should We Defend Born and Unborn Children with Force?* He based this on his previously published paper, *Was the Killing of Dr. Gunn Just? A Call to Defensive Action.* Hill wrote, "A brutal paid killer of hundreds upon hundreds of innocent unborn children was deterred by deadly force as he approached his latest victims. . . . If we say that one may justly trespass upon clinic property, upon what consistent biblical principle may we say that destroying clinic property requires a civil official. . . . Should we not therefore with zeal fired to a steady white glow, go forth to show forth God's righteous indignation upon those who defile with gruesome death children made in His image and likeness?"

The pro-violence anti-abortion movement is rooted in Operation Rescue's arguments for illegal, albeit nonviolent, civil disobedience. This led Hill to ask how Operation Rescue could justify its own illegal activity but reject the illegal activity he was proposing. After the murder of David Gunn, Don Treshman of Rescue America, another nationwide anti-abortion group, and Flip Benham of Operation Rescue demanded that all participants in their demonstrations sign a nonviolence pledge. Neither Treshman nor Benham recognized their self-contradiction. Their position says, in effect, "We will do violence to the law as we choose, but you must not do violence with which we disagree." The reality is this: once the pro-life movement moves beyond the threshold of illegal actions, there is no logical restraint on the level of illegality that can be employed in opposing abortion.

Paul Hill's "Defensive Action Declaration"

We, the undersigned, declare the justice of taking all godly action necessary to defend innocent human life including the use of force. We proclaim that whatever force is legitimate to defend the life of a born child is legitimate to defend the life of an unborn child.

We assert that if Michael Griffin did in fact kill David Gunn, his use of lethal force was justifiable provided it was carried out for the purpose of defending the lives of unborn children. Therefore, he ought to be acquitted of the charges against him.On September 6, 1993, Hill circulated his "defensive action declaration," which he invited others to sign. By September 20, eight people had signed this document and it had been distributed to hundreds of others. In August 1994, after Hill had murdered an abortionist and his escort, the *Washington Post* reported that thirty-two people had signed the document. The *Post* reported, "most leaders . . . still stand by the petition that 32 of them signed last year at Hill's request declaring that murdering abortion providers is 'justifiable homicide.'"

The Leading Advocates

The Reverend Michael Bray was among the signers of Hill's Defensive Action Statement. He is co-pastor of a Reformation Lutheran church in Bowie, Maryland. Bray was imprisoned between 1985 and 1989 following his conviction for conspiracy in the destruction of seven abortion facilities in the District of Columbia, Maryland, Virginia, and Delaware.[1] He is the author of two books, *When Bricks Bleed I'll Cry*[2] and *A Time to Kill*.[3] Bray has been a public supporter of Michael Griffin and Paul Hill after their acts of violence. In October 1994, Bray debated the proposition "Is the killing of abortion providers just?" with this author in Columbia, Maryland.

Father David Trosch, pastor of St. John the Baptist Catholic Church at Magnolia Springs, Alabama, surfaced as a major advocate of violence in August 1994. He was quoted as saying, "If 100 doctors need to die to save over one million babies a year, I see it as a fair trade." Trosch further said, "In a relatively short period of time, there will be a sufficient number of people who will have picked up on what Michael Griffin has done and start a national—perhaps an international—holocaust. Everything is in position for it to happen."[4]

Trosch founded Justifiable Homicide. This organization's stationery carries the comment, "Justifiable Homicide encourages 'God's Choice, a Live Baby not a Dead Baby. We are a very small part of what one day will populate the galaxy and universe.'" One of his publications, *In Defense of Others,* states, "In the wake of these two events [the killing of David Gunn and the shooting of George Tiller], Christians are called to critically examine the use of force, even potentially lethal force, to stop acts of abortion."[5]

In a July 25, 1994, letter to Media Associates Resource Coalition, Inc., Trosch wrote: "One of the most evil of beliefs is that a murderer of innocent children should not have his or her life terminated when extinction of his life would save, at least for the time being, the lives of innocent persons." [6] He had already examined this "critical issue" and concluded that "the killing of abortion providers is right." [7]

Archbishop Oscar H. Lipscomb of Mobile, Alabama, dismissed Trosch from his parish church and silenced him, but Trosch refused to submit to the church's discipline. Soon thereafter Lipscomb spelled out his own position, as opposed to Trosch's thinking, in a paper entitled "What Kind of Kingdom?" At present, Trosch is actively promoting violence against abortion providers and soliciting support from Roman Catholics.

Archbishop Lipscomb and the Peaceable Kingdom

In contrast to earthly kingdoms and the history of violence that has too often been their hallmark, the Kingdom of Christ, drawing from His victory over sin, is, above all, a peaceable kingdom. . . . Recently there has been much publicity given to an erroneous teaching about the Kingdom—as if it could be somehow defended by violence against others. . . . In response to the position that taking the life of abortionists is 'justifiable homicide,' I am issuing a pastoral instruction on the moral evil of murder . . .

The 1973 *Roe* and *Doe* decisions of the United States Supreme Court effectively stripped unborn children of the protection of law. . . . The Second Vatican Council proclaimed the Church's conviction that: 'from the moment of its conception life must be guarded with the greatest care . . . abortion and infanticide are unspeakable crimes.' . . . Many Americans promptly organized opposition to the *Roe* and *Doe* decisions within the framework of law. . . .

Some zealous opponents of abortion have been moved . . . to replace efforts to limit [abortions] spread within the frame of law with direct action against abortion taken in violation of the law. Some abortion clinics have been destroyed; persons providing or receiving abortions have been harassed. but most alarming has been violence against physicians known for performing abortions. . . . Some persons, even some priests, have attempted to defend such killing as 'justifiable homicide.' . . .

St. Augustine makes clear [that] to take the life of a wrongdoer without being authorized by public authority is to commit a homicide, an unjustified killing . . . what becomes of the rights of each person if public authority itself cannot or will not protect even so fundamental a right as that to life—especially the life of an innocent child in its mother's womb? The solution to such a situation cannot be to loose armed private persons to wreak vengeance on abortionists. Nor can it be to permit private persons to take up arms to prevent abortions. . . . Violence employed to control violence will only add to the evil of violence all too prevalent in our world today.

"YOU SHALL NOT MURDER—
A PASTORAL INSTRUCTION ON THIS MORAL
TEACHING OF THE CATHOLIC CHURCH,"
ARCHBISHOP OSCAR H. LIPSCOMB,
NOVEMBER 21, 1993.

On June 20, 1994, Trosch wrote Joseph Cardinal Ratzinger, head of the Vatican's Congregation for the

Doctrine of the Faith, asking him ten questions, including: Does a preborn person, from the moment of conception, have the right to life and to self-defense and protection by one or more other persons from unquestionable unjust aggression as does a fully grown, born person? . . . Is the killing of an active abortionist, by a person of right motivation and intent, "Justifiable Homicide?" [8]

After the December 30, 1994, murders in Massachusetts, the *New York Times* quoted Trosch as saying, "Anyone in the war zone has to expect to be part of the war that's going on." [9] On January 1, 1995, the *Times* reported: "The Rev. David Trosch, a Catholic priest from Alabama who has been relieved of his duties by the Church for his radical defense of the 'justifiable homicide' of abortion providers, mailed a letter to members of Congress last July, predicting [the] 'massive killing of abortionists and their staffs.' The letter also outlined a 'target list,' including members of the American Civil Liberties Union, Planned Parenthood and the National Organization for Women, saying they would be 'sought out and terminated as vermin are terminated.' " [10]

The Second Murder and Then Terrorism

The shooting of Dr. John Bayard Britton and James Barrett in July 1994 and the murder of two abortion-clinic receptionists in December 1994 demonstrated that these were not isolated incidences. While they were not a part of an organized conspiracy, they did represent a changing mentality in one element of the pro-life movement. From the March 1993 murder of an abortionist and the August 1993 wounding of an abortionist, the violence expanded to the July 1994 murder of an abortionist and his escort. Before the July 1994 attack only abortionists themselves had been assaulted, but now a companion had been murdered.

The December 30, 1994, murder of two abortion-clinic receptionists at Brookline, Massachusetts, widened the terrorism. Kansas abortionist, Dr. George Tiller, himself the victim of a violent assault in 1993, told *Time* magazine, "The turning point in our profession occurred last week . . . when innocent bystanders, as it were, were slaughtered."[11]

Because of the massive media attention that Hill received, some pro-life advocates commented on the responsibility of the media for tacitly encouraging Hill: "Unfortunately, over the past year, many in the media— including *USA Today,* the *New York Times* and *NBC Nightly News*—have given Hill a national spotlight, providing him undeserved attention and likely increasing delusions of self importance. . . . The media has also created the illusion that he represents a constituency within the pro-life movement."[12]

The July 1994 murders in Pensacola provoked reactions from many sources. Everyone attempted to grapple with the question of responsibility, "Who is to blame?" The *New York Times* blamed the entire pro-life movement:

> [W]hen you tell your followers that abortion is "murder," that doctors are "baby killers," that America has an "abortion holocaust," you cannot so neatly disavow responsibility once someone takes you at your word. The hysterical rhetoric of the anti-abortion movement in this country is an invitation to violence.
>
> And this is more than rhetoric. Operation Rescue and other groups have used physical obstruction and all kinds of harassment to terrify patients and doctors at clinics. . . . Opposition to abortion is a position that everyone should respect.[13]

The *Times* correctly pointed out the relationship between the illegal, nonviolent activities of Operation

Rescue and the illegal, violent activities of the pro-violence, anti-abortionists. Yet the *Times* makes no comment about the "hysterical rhetoric" of the pro-choice and/or pro-abortion forces. Emotionalism on both sides has contributed to the present circumstances, and both sides are responsible for the emotionalism. In a March 21, 1993, newspaper column, this writer said: "Conviction should not require distortion in order to sustain its commitment. Both sides of this debate would better serve their goals by focusing upon facts and reality, rather than manipulating the emotions of their followers. Convictions seldom lead to violence; emotionalism almost always results in violence." [14]

The *Washington Post* gave a more balanced response than the *Times:* "The more difficult problem is not prosecuting these cases but preventing them. . . . Two steps might make a real difference. The large majority of abortion opponents who abhor violence must speak out, not only after an atrocity but continually. . . . It is not enough to disclaim responsibility after doctors and clinic volunteers have been murdered. There is a positive responsibility to direct protest, to counsel colleagues who appear ready to cross the line to violence and to cooperate with law enforcement officials in applying sanctions early when possible." [15]

Nationally syndicated columnist Paul Greenberg condemned the violence, but he argued that the entire pro-life movement was not to blame. Greenberg said:

> There will always be those who make political hay out of terror. Predictably enough, they will use acts of violence like this one at Pensacola to tar the whole anti-abortion movement. . . . The unfairness of this tack would be evident even if various anti-abortion spokesmen didn't consistently denounce all such crimes every chance they get. Most of these people would not

be fighting abortion if they cared nothing for human life, including that of their political opponents. . . . To blame critics of abortion for being 'unwilling or unable to control the violent extremists' that not even the police or US marshals seem able to control. . . . Well, that's just one more of the rhetorical shots in this political dispute over very real life."[16]

Many must share responsibility for escalating violence in the anti-abortion movement. Zealots on both sides of the question have emotionalized the issues, making dispassionate discussions of substance almost impossible. The media has capitalized on the hysteria of those who make "good" headlines. More responsible pro-life advocates have failed to articulate a theology of opposing abortion, which would give direction and limits to those driven by emotion. All of these share the responsibility for the current situation, and all must participate in moving the debate—both in support and in opposition—beyond this point.

In August 1993, this writer asked Paul Hill if he would kill an abortion provider. He said, "I have no plans to." But on July 29, 1994, Hill shot and killed Dr. John B. Britton and his escort, James Herman Barrett. Just as Hill was courted by the press after the murder of David Gunn, Michael Bray has been in the media spotlight since the murder of Britton. Trosch and Bray are now the principal spokesmen in the United States for anti-abortion violence.

On September 21, 1994, the Christian Life Commission of the Southern Baptist Convention issued a twelve-page statement on violence in the anti-abortion movement. It stated in part, "We believe that the point of view of persons advocating violence against abortion doctors requires serious moral reflection and engagement, more serious than has thus far publicly occurred. . . . Lack of serious engagement with the views of persons who advocate the use of violence will only increase the risk that this drift will occur." [17] This statement, like Archbishop Lipscomb's earlier, clearly rejects the pro-violence position, but neither deals in detail with the arguments used to justify that position. Additionally, neither identifies the relationship between the nonviolent civil disobedience of Operation Rescue and the violent civil disobedience of the pro-violence anti-abortionists.

Demonstrating the confusion in the thinking of the advocates of violence, Michael Bray states: "Are you advocating the murder of doctors? No, on three counts. First, we are not talking about 'doctors' but about hired childkillers. Second, we are not talking, therefore, about murder, but about homicide. . . . We simply declare that the slaying of . . . government-sanctioned childkillers is justifiable." [18] This sophistry tries to hide the real nature of the act by calling it something else. It attempts to confuse the fundamental ethical question with verbal gymnastics. Regardless of what you call another human being, you cannot dehumanize him to the point of justifying his murder, even if you believe he is a murderer.

Many Are Confused

Perhaps the greatest evidence of the need for a thorough refutation of Bray's position and of other pro-violence anti-abortionists is the endorsement of *A Time to Kill* by Professor Carl Laney of Western Conservative Baptist Seminary. Laney said, "This book presents a rather convincing argument for the use of force in the defense of the unborn. I find myself on the horns of a personal dilemma in this regard. I have some personal conscience issues that would prevent me from the active use of force. Yet I would not condemn those whose conscience has led them in the other direction. I hope this book receives the serious attention it deserves."[19] It is difficult to believe that Laney, who is otherwise a careful and creditable scholar, read and understood what Bray advocates.

At the October 1994 debate in Columbia, Maryland, the positions taken by Bray and his supporters revealed that they have given serious thought to revolution, terrorism, and violence. Some openly discussed their belief in the need for revolution. One well-intentioned anti-abortionist said to this writer, "Do you believe in the Declaration of Independence?" He then said, "There are stronger grounds for revolting against the government today than existed in 1776!" When asked, "Who would you revolt against?" there was no answer. There was only a visceral desire to do something, even if it was the wrong thing. These otherwise good people are driven by their passions. They desperately need the counsel of sound, biblical teaching. Some are teachable, and therefore reachable. Others need their influence diminished by a thorough refutation of their position.

Sympathy with the advocates and perpetrators of anti-abortion violence was evidenced across America. On August 28, 1994, newspapers across the country reported that Regent University Law School planned to publish an article in their *Law Review* that purported to provide a defense for Michael Griffin in his trial for the murder of David Gunn.[20] The article entitled, "Use of Force in Defense of Another: An Argument for Michael Griffin" was withdrawn from publication only after Paul Hill's actions on July 29, 1994. The author of the brief stated: "Throughout history, individuals, like Griffin, who have intervened in defense of others have been exonerated . . . positive law is not a shield to prosecution for government agents who enforce unlawful laws. The Rule of Law condemns those who act in conformity with positive law and exonerates those who intervene in violation of positive law. . . . Michael Griffin shot abortionist David Gunn in defense of ten unborn children. . . . He acted to prevent an imminent, future [harm]. . . . The case law requirements for justification of his actions are satisfied."[21]

The December 4, 1994, issue of the *Houston Post* contained an article entitled, "Texas Klan As Divergent As Its Two Dominant Personalities." In that article the leader of the Knights of the White Camellia said, "his Klan is a law-abiding group, but adds that there can be such a thing as 'positive violence.'" To prove his case, the klansman cited the abortion doctor killed in Florida. He said, "We don't promote violence, but I don't see that as wrong." If the KKK cites the pro-violence anti-abortionists to justify its own acts of terrorism, others will begin using the same arguments unless those arguments are refuted.

A Necessary Response

How do Christians respond to these questions?

- What should Christians do when their government forces them to pay taxes that are used to pay for abortions?

- Why were the Nazis tried at Nuremberg for not resisting evil? Why shall we not be tried in the same way if we do not forcefully resist abortion?

- Is it ever appropriate for Christians to use civil disobedience and/or force?

- Why can the United States ask Christians to forswear violence?

- How do you apply the Old Testament law to twentieth-century America?

- When is it right, just, and biblical for Christians to appeal to a "higher law" and therefore disobey the laws of the land in which they live?

- Who has the right to initiate capital punishment against a human being for the breaking of God's law?

- How does the fact that the United States is not a theocracy affect the application of the Old Testament to twentieth-century America?

- What should Christians do to oppose abortion and violence?

Here are some of the reasons responsible Christian leaders should formulate a Christlike response to this violence:

- The rising tide of anti-abortion violence.

- Publication and endorsement of Michael Bray's book, *A Time to Kill.*

- The media attention that Bray is receiving, just as Hill previously received.

- Operation Rescue's advocacy of nonviolent, illegal activities against abortion clinics and abortion providers.

- The unanswered questions about Christian responsibility to oppose evil in a democratic republic and how that responsibility is to be carried out.

- Claims that America deserves revolution because of abortion on demand.

Answering these and other pertinent questions is the task of this book.

2

SANCTITY OF HUMAN LIFE

RED AND YELLOW, BLACK AND WHITE, they are precious in His sight" are the words to a song many children learn in Vacation Bible School. The basis of this song is the absolute value of every human life in the sight of God. The Hippocratic Oath affirms that a physician is never to do harm to an unborn child, even if he is offered a reward for doing so. Some may find this surprising since it is an occultic oath to a false god, but Western culture has always affirmed the high value of human life and has extended that value to the unborn child. Many people are questioning this fundamental cultural assumption. The attack on the sanctity of human life has led to the loss of a sense of self-worth by many men and women. As long as one was the special creation of a personal God, it was simple to imagine that one is important. Once society became sufficiently secular to cast doubt on the proposition that man is the special creation of a personal God, however, a poor self-image became a common problem among men and women.

Sanctity of Life under Attack

The attack on the sanctity of human life, which resulted in abortion-on-demand, has also resulted in many nations entertaining euthanasia as a national policy. In 1984,

Richard Lamm, governor of Colorado, scandalized the nation with his "Duty to Die" speech. He asserted that old people should not have extensive health resources expended upon them.[1] The Clinton administration's healthcare reform act proposed that "terminal expenses" be limited for elderly citizens. At the root of the rationing of healthcare resources is a low view of the value of individuals when their interests seem to conflict with those of the masses. Dr. Jack Kevorkian has become notorious for "assisted" suicides.[2] The *Los Angeles Times* reported that Mensa, an organization formed by those with high IQ's, published the following statement in its Los Angeles chapter's November 1994 newsletter, *Lament:*

> Those people who are so mentally defective that they cannot live in society should, as soon as they are identified as defective, be humanely dispatched. . . . [Adolf Hitler's] actions prevent a rational discussion of the creation of the master race . . . society must face the concept that we kill off the old, weak, the stupid and the inefficient. . . . It is not clear to me just exactly why anyone would expend time and effort and money on the homeless. What good are they? The vast majority are too stupid, too lazy, too crazy, or too anti-social to earn a living. . . . The rest of the homeless should be humanely done away with, like abandoned kittens. . . . A piece of meat in the shape of a man but without a mind is not a human being, whether the body be deadly ill, damaged by accident, mentally blank because of brain deficiency, or criminally insane.[3]

Abortion and euthanasia are bookend results of the loss of belief in the sanctity of human life. *Roe v. Wade* is the result of the attack on the value of unborn human life in the United States. Christians should work toward the reversal of this decision, but we must recognize two important facts: legalization did not create abortion in America and its criminalization will not ultimately solve the problem.

The reality of the attack on the sanctity of human life was declared by an editorial in the prestigious journal *Pediatrics*. The moral relativism of this quotation should have alarmed many people, but not one voice was raised in opposition to this statement in subsequent issues of the journal. This fact and the editorial itself establish beyond question that the issue of the sanctity of human life is under attack.

Dr. Peter Singer and the Sanctity of Life

The ethical outlook that holds human life to be sacrosanct—I shall call it "the sanctity-of-life view"—is under attack. The first major blow to the sanctity-of-life view was the spreading acceptance of abortion throughout the Western world. . . . A second blow to the sanctity-of-life view has been the revelation that it is standard practice in many major public hospitals to refrain from providing necessary life-saving treatment to certain patients. . . . Is the erosion of the sanctity-of-life view really so alarming? Change is often, in itself, alarming, especially change in something that for centuries has been spoken of in such hushed tones that to question it is automatically to commit sacrilege. . . . Once the religious mumbo-jumbo surrounding the term "human" has been stripped away, we may continue to see normal members of our species as possessing greater capacities of rationality, self-consciousness, communication, and so on, than members of any other species; but we will not regard as sacrosanct the life of each and every member of our species, no matter how limited its capacity for intelligent or even conscious life may be. If we compare a severely defective human infant with a non-human animal, a dog or a pig, for example, we will often find the non-human animal to have superior capacities, both actual and potential for rationality, self consciousness, communication and anything else that can plausibly be considered morally significant. Only the fact that the defective infant is a member of the species *Homo sapiens* leads it to be treated differently from the dog or pig. Species membership alone, however, is not morally relevant. Humans who bestow superior value on the lives of all human beings, solely because they are members of our own species, are judging along lines strikingly similar to those used by white racists who bestow superior value on the lives of other whites, merely because they are members of their own race. . . . If we can put aside the obsolete and erroneous notion of the sanctity of all human life, we may start to look at human life as it really is: at the quality of life that each human being has or can achieve.

PETER SINGER,
PEDIATRICS, 72, NO. 1
(JULY 1983): 128–29.

The ethical position from which the assertions in this editorial are drawn are devoid of any concept of God. Today many well-intentioned people reject the Judeo-Christian ethical system upon which the United States of America was founded. These men and women argue that they are attempting to rid society of superstition, racism, and ignorance, but they are, in fact, working to establish an Orwellian 1984 nightmare in our land by the year 2000.

All Life Is Sacred

Fundamentally, the sanctity of human life derives from the sanctity of all life. Proverbs 12:10 states: "A righteous man regardeth the life of his beast: but the tender mercies of the wicked are cruel." The association of the humane treatment of animals with the effect of righteousness—the character of God—in a man's life indicates God's valuation of all life. No life can be maliciously or capriciously used for the amusement of another without regard to the welfare and/or value of that life. Concern for the survival of whales seems hypocritical in the face of mass abortion of human babies. Yet a biblical world-view would support "save the whale" efforts while also supporting opposition to abortion.

While animals may be used for the benefit of mankind, either for labor or for food, the law of God required that man not ignore the welfare of animals. Deuteronomy 25:4 states: "Thou shalt not muzzle the ox when he treadeth out the corn." Although God has placed a higher value on human life, no one can ignore the value of any life. The dominion that man was given over the animal world was to be exercised under the providence of God that is concerned for the welfare of all life.

"Dominion," the authority that man was given by God over the creation, did not excuse man from responsibility for how he dealt with the animal kingdom. Genesis 1:26 states, "and let them have dominion." *Dominion* translates a Hebrew word meaning "to subdue, to rule over." As will be seen below, one of the principle aspects of man's being created in the image of God is that he was created to rule as God rules—compassionately and with consideration of others.

God takes "pleasure" in His creation, but He does not "amuse" Himself with it. Revelation 4:11 states: "Thou art worthy, O Lord, to receive glory and honour and power: for thou hast created all things, and for thy pleasure they are and were created." *Pleasure* is gained in a relationship that is reciprocal, that is, in which the benefit of each party is considered in any transaction. *Amusement* allows one to use another for one's own benefit without regard for his welfare. God "pleasures" Himself in the creation, but He does not "amuse" Himself with His creatures. Man, created in the image of God—with the capacity to make decisions and to relate to other beings—is to conduct himself toward others as God conducts Himself, that is, with pleasure, but not with amusement. Therefore, cruelty to animals is forbidden by the sanctity of life, while the use of animals for the benefit of man, when done mercifully and frugally, is not.[4]

Human Life Is Unique

The sanctity of human life is also seen in the uniqueness of human life; namely, man is created in the image of God. Volumes are filled attempting to describe what this means. The phrase from Genesis 1:26, "Let us make man in our image, after our likeness," is filled with as much mystery as it is meaning. Certainly, it does not mean that man is a "little god." Man possesses none of the Godlike capacities of omnipresence, omnipotence, or of omniscience that characterize the true God. God, however, has given man a nature that distinguishes him from the lower animals.

Image is the translation of a Hebrew word meaning "an image, likeness, so called from its shadowing forth."

Likeness translates another Hebrew word meaning "similitude, likeness, image." The image of God distinguishes humanity from other creatures. While scholars differ over its exact meaning, the concept of man being created in the image of God certainly includes "man's likeness to God's intellectual and moral nature" and his "dominion over the world." [5]

Man, being in the image of God as to his capacity for responsibility, choice, loyalty, love, devotion, and obedience, means that man has inherent value that cannot be removed by any comparison with others. Genesis 1:26 clearly affirms the sanctity of human life. Life has absolute value, which cannot be made relative by any standard of measurement, whether of productivity, possessions, position, or power.

Moses' Law and the Sanctity of Life

Old Testament laws about murder and negligence further emphasize the sanctity of human life. In the Sixth Commandment, God commanded, "Thou shalt not kill" (Exod. 20:13), and the law of God commanded that murderers were to be put to death (Lev. 24:17). The law went into detail as to how to treat cases of death by negligence. Exodus 21:12–13 reveals that the central question in cases of homicide was premeditation. It states: "He that smiteth a man, so that he die, shall be surely put to death. And if a man lie not in wait, but God deliver him into his hand; then I will appoint thee a place whither he shall flee."

The law also prescribed a penalty for those guilty of another's death by *negligence* in Exodus 21:28–29. Any person, knowing that an animal they owned was dangerous, could not neglect the welfare of others by ignoring the aggressive or violent behavior of the animal. The basis of this commandment is the value of human life to God. The superior value of human life was seen in that a favorite animal could not be kept if it posed a danger to a stranger or even to one's enemy.

In the case of *injury*, Exodus 21:22–24 states: "If men strive, and hurt a woman with child, so that her fruit depart from her, and yet no mischief follow: he shall be surely punished, according as the woman's husband will lay upon him; and he shall pay as the judges determine. And if any mischief follow, then thou shalt give life for life, eye for eye, tooth for tooth, hand for hand, foot for foot." Here God affirms the value of the unborn life of a human being. No one could accidentally or intentionally harm the life of the unborn child without consequences.

The law prescribed narrow limits within which the covenant community could take the life of another. The instances in which a man's life may be taken by the community addressed offenses against the spirit of man, the body of man, and the soul of man. Offenses against the spirit of man, which would result in capital punishment in a theocracy, were God's judgment against witches and false prophets. Exodus 22:18 states: "Thou shalt not suffer a witch to live." The danger of man's indulgence in the occult was so great that those who encouraged such were to be eliminated from the theocratic society. Likewise, the false prophet was so dangerous to the spiritual health of God's people that he was to be put to death (Deut. 18:20; 13:2–4, 10). The theocratic government of ancient Israel was to put to death anyone who encouraged rebellion, disloyalty, idolatry, or abandonment of God.

How should we apply this in a nontheocratic society like the United States? God's people should oppose occultists (witches or false prophets) by exposing the error of their ways, their motives, and their methods. We must eliminate their influence, not by executing them, but by biblically renouncing their false teaching and practice.

Sanctity of the Unborn

Another evidence of the sanctity of human life and particularly of the unborn is the fact that God opens and closes the womb. He knows the child before he is born. The Bible repeatedly affirms that it is God who has control over conception:

- God foretold Samson's birth. An angel told his mother: "thou shalt conceive, and bear a son" (Judg. 13:5).

- Genesis 29:31 states, "And when the LORD saw that Leah was hated, he opened her womb: but Rachel was barren."

- 1 Samuel 1:5 reports, "But unto Hannah he gave a worthy portion; for he loved Hannah: but the LORD had shut up her womb."

- God called Jeremiah to be a prophet before his birth (Jer. 1:5).

- "Lo, children are an heritage of the LORD: and the fruit of the womb is his reward" (Ps. 127:3).

Modern science understands the mechanism of fertilization of the ovum by the sperm, which explains the process of "opening the womb." Science, however, does not know why pregnancy results at one time and not at another. Science can imitate conception, but it cannot, with prescience and wisdom, control all of the factors of conception. Only God opens and closes the womb, and this invests every pregnancy and therefore every child with absolute value.

Samson and the Sanctity of Life

Perhaps nothing in the Bible affirms the sanctity of human life like the life of Samson. Just as Samson's mother's womb was opened by God, Mary's womb was opened by God to give birth to the Messiah. In a number of ways Samson's life foreshadowed the coming Messiah, but in one way his life particularly foreshadowed the mission of Jesus Christ. That was in his death.[6] The Bible declares that Samson, who voluntarily offered himself as a sacrifice to God, killed more enemies in his death than he had ever done in his life (Judg. 16:30). This is the message concerning the life and death of our Lord Jesus Christ in Hebrews 2:14–18. Just as Samson's conception was foretold by the Lord, so the Messiah's conception and birth was prophesied (Isa. 7:14). The sanctity of human life was affirmed by the fact that the Messiah was to be a human being while at the same time being God.

Ordained from the Womb

The Hebrew aversion to abortion arose from the expectation of the birth of the Messiah. No woman would have an abortion when the seed she bore might be God's Lamb. It was God who initiated the process of the incarnation of Himself in the person of the Son of God. It is God who is always the initiator of conception. The fact that God opens and closes the womb in His sovereign foreknowledge precludes any interference with pregnancy for any reason.

No Christian woman now expects the birth of the Messiah, but every woman can expect the birth of a man or woman of God, someone who will be used of God to call His people to righteousness. Every pregnancy has the potential to produce a great servant of God. This invests every child with absolute value.

God not only ordained the opening of the womb of Samson's mother, He also ordained Samson's features in the womb, further demonstrating the sanctity of human life, as the very features of the child are sovereignly ordained by God for His purposes. Among the most significant features of a person is gender. God's design for a person's function in the kingdom of God upon earth is largely determined by sex. Furthermore, if God foreknows, thereby predetermining the sex of a child, then He foreknows and predetermines every feature of a child.

A Son, Not Just a Male

God did not tell Samson's mother that she would have a "male"; He revealed she would have a "son." *Sonship* bespeaks paternity, indicating a relationship that is more than biological. It bespeaks particularity, indicating uniqueness of resources available to each person, rather than being just one of a number. It also denotes personality, indicating uniqueness of responses to one's environment and stimuli. Manoah's wife was to have a child, not an "it." He was a son though he was yet unborn. If the child was ever a child in the womb, he is always a child in the womb.

Samson's father gave an interesting reply to the angel: "Now let thy words come to pass. How shall we order the child, and how shall we do unto him?" (Judg. 13:12). The word translated *order* means "verdict or judgment, a sentence or formal decree of divine law." Manoah asked what God's judgment of this child's life shall be. That judgment—God's plan for Samson's life—invested his life with value and sanctity. God has such a judgment, such an order, for every human life on this earth, thereby giving every human life value and sanctity (Rom. 12:1–2; Eph. 2:10).

Do translates *asah,* a Hebrew word meaning "to do or to make, furnish, deck, dress." Manoah understood that God had a plan for his son's life; now he wanted to know how he could participate in that plan. Manoah asked how he was to "furnish," or "dress" the life of this child to facilitate the fulfilling of God's plan. The sanctity of human life not only precludes the aborting of a child, it includes the responsibility to impact the child's spiritual life positively in teaching him to adore and obey God. God's responsibility was to have a plan for each child's life; man's responsibility is to help every child discover and fulfill that plan.

Parental Responsibility from Conception

God's response indicates that the parents' responsibility for the child begins at conception: "She may not eat of any thing that cometh of the vine, neither let her drink wine or strong drink, nor eat any unclean thing: all that I commanded her let her observe" (Judg. 13:14). Even the qualifications of the child to be a Nazarite[7] began at conception. Clearly this "product of conception" was a child with eternal consequences for those who would abuse him, because whatever went into the mother affected the child, not only physically as an organism (the product of conception), but spiritually as an individual with the attributes and essentials of a real person.

Judges 13:14 also affirms that God's design for the child includes his parents, who are accountable to God for how they discharge their responsibility. The father's equal and, by other revelation, greater responsibility for the child was indicated when Manoah asked, "how shall we do unto him?" (Judg. 13:12).

God not only formed and fashioned Samson in the womb,[8] He formed and fashioned all men and women, thus investing every human being's life with sanctity. Isaiah 43:1 observes, "But now thus saith the LORD that created thee, O Jacob, and he that formed thee, O Israel, Fear not: for I have redeemed thee, I have called thee by thy name; thou art mine."

Let's notice two important Hebrew words. *Created* translates the Hebrew word *bara,* which means "created out of nothing." God's design of each person is an act of creative energy and genius, like that exercised in the creation of the heavens and the earth. Even when in man's estimate there are deficiencies in a person's physical, mental, or emotional makeup, God has an eternal purpose for them (see Rom. 8:28). *Formed* translates the Hebrew word *yatsar,* meaning "to squeeze into a shape, fashion, form, to narrow, to determine." God not only conceived of the image of a person by His sovereign design, He then brought together the forces both physical and spiritual that fashioned in them His design (see also Jer. 33:1–3).

Isaiah 44:2 observes, "Thus saith the LORD that made thee, and formed thee from the womb, which will help thee; Fear not, O Jacob, my servant; and thou, Jesurun, whom I have chosen." The word translated *formed* is *yatsar,* also found in Isaiah 43:1 above. It is used of the molding of clay into the design conceived by the potter and is translated *made* in Judges 13:12, when Manoah asked God for instructions for dealing with his son. *Yatsar* speaks of God's work; *asah* speaks of man's work. As both responsibilities— God's design and the father's diligence—are undertaken, the ultimate product is honoring to God.

The Word of God goes further in confirming that Samson and every other child in the womb is a real person. Isaiah 49:1 states: "Listen, O isles, unto me; and hearken, ye people, from far; The LORD hath called me from the womb; from the bowels of my mother hath he made mention of my name." *Called* translates *qara,* meaning "to address by name," and only persons are addressed by name. Only the Messiah shall have a name that is above every name. There is no animal or inanimate object in the Bible that is assigned a personal name by God. That which God calls by name is human and has the sanctity of life.

Samson's Prenatal Care

The sanctity of Samson's life is further seen by the fact that his mission in life was assigned prior to his conception and the requirements of that assignment were to be observed

28

while he was in the womb. Judges 13:5 declares that Samson would be a Nazarite. The actions of his mother before his birth would affect his service to God after his birth, because God had called Samson to be a Nazarite. This fact alone confirmed that Samson was fully and wholly a person from conception. No subhuman being was called to be a Nazarite.

If Samson's mother drank wine, it would defile the Nazarite in her womb. God's instructions to her established the personhood of the unborn Samson (Judg. 13:3–5). Not only does food and beverage affect the baby, along with other ingested things, by transplacental movement, but the emotions of the mother and father, words spoken to the child, songs sung to the child, and prayers prayed for the child will affect him or her in the womb. There were no dietary laws for animals or things, only for people. Therefore, the requirement to restrict certain foods— wine and that which is unclean—from the mother's diet in order not to defile the child is absolute evidence that this is a baby, a human child from conception, and not an "it."

Whether in the womb or after birth, the sanctity of human life invests each child with value. The sanctity of human life gives every human confidence that God cares about each person. This confidence ought to protect the child in the womb from attack, and it ought to comfort parents that God's care for their child continues even in their absence.

God's commandments were directed toward preserving, restoring, and sustaining man's relationship with God. There was never a commandment given that had as its purpose the establishment of a relationship between God and an animal or between God and an object. The form of the answer to Manoah's question in Judges 13:12 also affirmed that this was a child. Manoah's answer from the angel of the Lord was in the form of a commandment, not a request or a suggestion. The violation of a commandment is sin; the violation of the personhood of the unborn child is sin. That a commandment, not a suggestion or a recommendation, but a commandment was given concerning this "product of conception" is absolute proof that God considered this "product" a human being with full moral responsibilities and eternal purposes.

If this "product" were a child, then all "products of conception" are children. If one child may be legitimately destroyed by abortion, then all children can be legitimately destroyed by abortion. If abortion is ever right, then it is always right. In that the aborting of the child Samson would have been sin, it is always sin to abort any child.

God said of Samson before he was conceived, "and he shall begin to deliver Israel out of the hand of the Philistines" (Judg. 13:5b). God did not say "it" would begin to deliver Israel; He said "he" will begin to deliver Israel. It was not "a" man that would bring deliverance to Israel, it was *this* man—this specific, special, and significant man. It was this man who was a man from his mother's womb. In this way also, Samson was like the Messiah. The Messiah would not be just anyone; He would be Jesus Christ, who was known of His Father, from the womb.

Luke 2:21 states: "And when eight days were accomplished for the circumcising of the child, his name was called JESUS, which was so named of the angel before he was conceived in the womb." One does not name a blob of protoplasm; one does not name a "fetus." One names a human being, a child, as God named the Messiah and as He named Samson.

The fact that God appoints a specific person limits the one delineated by that appointment to the human race, because God did not use specific, special, or significant animals. Any animal would do. It might have to have certain characteristics, but no animal had to have a specific identity.

Samson, like Jesus, was a human being from his conception, for all of the reasons given above.

Each Child Is Special

Early in gestation, it is impossible to determine physically the sex of a child. At about six weeks, sexual differentiation begins, and the sex of a child is observable. Before this event, God knows the sex of the child and has already predetermined that sex. While science knows that an XX chromosome produces a girl and a XY produces a boy, science does not know why one family has five boys and another has five girls. The fact that man can discern patterns in God's providence does not empower man to control or change His providence. The general laws of biology, while valid and helpful in large groups, are of no help in determining particulars in individual cases. Those general laws of biology do not invalidate the providence of God or His sovereignty in human events.

God's special creation and design of each human being invests in each person a value beyond any function that he or she may or may not perform. God's design of each unchangeable feature creates in man a gratitude for God's love and care, even when we might not understand all of the reasons for how things are. God's purpose in being so intimately involved in the conception, design, and birth of His children is that they may know their worth and have a redemptive and creative positive self-esteem.

The world associates self-worth with what you can produce or achieve. The world's method of establishing self-esteem has failed. Educators have learned that about 80 percent of all students entering school feel good about themselves and have a positive self-image. By the fifth grade, only 20 percent have high self-esteem. By the time students are in the twelfth grade, fewer than 5 percent feel good about themselves and have a positive self-image. The sanctity of human life produces self-worth, as a person knows that he is the special creation of a personal God. The rejection of the sanctity of human life, the very basis of abortion, produces self-doubt and rejection of self. Self-doubt and self-rejection ultimately produces in men and women the desperation from which abortion comes.

God designed man with a "natural" love, with a spontaneous, instinctive love for his offspring. One of the evidences of the fall of man and of the approach of the end times, Paul declared in 2 Timothy 3:3, is that men will be "without natural affection." Man will be without the God-given, God-designed affection for their offspring and for their parents. One of the evidences of the sanctity of human life is this affection—the love that a man or woman has for a child in the womb whom they have not seen or held. One of the evidences of the approach of God's final judgment is that men and women are able to reject the loving of the child in the womb, treat the child as an "it," and kill that child for their own convenience.

A Mother's Prayers

The sanctity of human life has significance before we are born and after we are dead. A number of years ago, one of my young patients conceived. During her pregnancy she had to have two major abdominal operations. Shortly after delivery, she was discovered to have inoperable and terminal cancer. The day that I told them of her diagnosis, she and her husband prayed to receive Christ as their personal Savior. Subsequently, as her health deteriorated, this young lady expressed one great fear, "What will happen to my baby after I am gone?"

This mother had endured a nightmare of pain to bring this child into this world. Now she feared that her death would leave her child in danger. Based on the sanctity of human life—of God's care for that baby in the mother's womb and of His concern for every aspect of that child's life—I counseled her, "Pray for your child. Pray for his teachers. Pray for his friends. Pray for his mate and for his career. Pray for his love for God. And long after you have gone to be with the Lord, God Himself will be working in your child's life to fulfill the petitions that you have stored up for him."

My son and I flew across country to conduct the funeral of this mother. At the memorial service, I said, "In the ensuing months, as Mary [not her real name] was anxious, not about her death, but about leaving her child behind, I encouraged her to spend the hours laying in bed to pray through his life. Our Heavenly Father would continue to answer [these prayers] even when she is in heaven with Him. So Joe [not his real name], as you go through kindergarten and have a particularly helpful and pleasant teacher, know it is because a godly mother, in her last days upon this earth, besought her Heavenly Father to attend to your needs, which she could not be physically present to provide . . . every good thing that happens to you will be a gift of your Heavenly Father, often given because of the prayers of your mother." God did not cause this young mother to have cancer, but He had a plan for her life that cancer could not defeat, and He has a plan for her child's life—fashioned while the child was in his mother's womb—that the providence of God will sustain and fulfill in her.

Summary

Now let's summarize the most important ideas of this chapter about the sanctity of human life.

1. The sanctity of human life is under attack from abortion and euthanasia.

2. All life is precious to God.

3. The Bible establishes the value of human life to God by:

- affirming that man is created in the image of God

- holding man accountable for taking human life

- placing limitations on capital punishment

- setting forth the extent to which God's people should go to preserve human life

- subordinating the importance of all religious obligations to caring for others

4. The life of Samson establishes the sanctity of human life because:

- God opens and closes the womb

- Samson's life foreshadows the coming of the Savior, and every child has the potential of being a servant of God

- Samson was to be a son, not an "it"

- God gives parents "natural affection" for their offspring, even before the child is born

- Samson was not to be just a "male," he was to be a "son," indicating paternity, personality, and particularity

- Samson's parents' responsibility began at conception

- God only gives names to people

- Samson was a Nazarite from his mother's

womb; only human beings are Nazarites

- Samson's mother's actions, while he was in the womb, would affect his service to God later

- Commandments are only given to human beings

- God's outline of a divine purpose for Samson, while in his mother's womb, indicated his personhood

5. Children are persons from their conception because every child is born with a sin nature, and the Bible never holds animals morally accountable for their conduct.

6. All human life is precious to God from conception.

7. All human life is sanctified by the concern God exercises toward that life.

8. God hates abortion because, more than any other human act, it denies the sanctity of human life.

9. God also hates abortion because those who abort judge themselves superior and the aborted child to be inferior.

As we reject violence in opposing abortion and as we examine how Christians should oppose abortion, the foundation upon which every concept is built is the absolute value of every human life.

3

OPERATION RESCUE

IT WAS A LONG, HOT SUMMER in 1991. More than two thousand protesters were arrested for obstructing the entrance to Dr. George Tiller's Wichita abortion clinic. Two years before Tiller had been shot and wounded, the level of confrontation began rising and a segment of the pro-life movement took a violent turn. Believers started asking themselves:

- Is civil disobedience a biblically-sound method for the pro-life movement to employ at this time?

- Are the actions of Operation Rescue appropriate when viewed from a biblical perspective?

Why does Operation Rescue confuse so many Christians? Many believers confuse the theocratic life they live in God's kingdom with the democratic life they live before the government. If the arguments of "being under authority" were removed from Romans 13, there is no biblical imperative for obstructing the rights of others to live within the constraints of a democratic society, even when they have rejected the reign of God over their lives.

A theocratic society like ancient Israel would put abortionists to death. In our democratic society, the majority must rule. This is why many immoral and unethical acts are legal. Many things are ungodly and unrighteous but legal. Abortion is only one example. Pornography is another, and you can make your own list. Remember, however, that because abortion is legal, it is by definition not criminal.

Our government allows abortion but does not *mandate* it, at least not at the present. Abortion is only allowed. This is an important distinction. If, as in China, abortion were mandated by law, a nonviolent action similar to Operation Rescue would be the imperative response for all believers. In that abortion is not mandated—no one is required to have an abortion—our proper response is protesting, not picketing. Even God Almighty allows men to walk in the counsel of their own hearts (Ps. 81:11–12) until His judgment against the evil of that heart is full (Ps. 94:13).

Our protest should be like Jonah's work, the prophetic and passionate preaching of God's promised judgment upon those who persist in rebelling against Him and His way. To protest—to preach, to publicize, and to prophesy against—that which is legal but immoral and ungodly is to stand in the tradition of the prophets of Israel and the men of God throughout the ages. To picket—to obstruct the free course of those who, even while rebelling against God's commandments, are nonetheless in compliance with the law of the land—requires the minority to arrogate to itself a right that it does not have in a democracy. In our lexicon, protesting declares that what another is doing is wrong, and it warns them that they should not do it. Picketing declares that we disagree with what another is doing and we will use force to prevent them from doing it.

A democratic republic gives no minority the right to impose its views on the majority by coercion or force. Yet all minorities have the right to expect the majority not to require them to violate their deeply held religious convictions in order to comply with the law. This is the trade-off. The individual cannot forcefully impose his religious convictions upon others, but the institution cannot require the individual to violate those convictions. When either violates this social contract, it is coercion and the proper response changes.

Operation Rescue argues that current law allows coercive force to be exercised against the baby in the uterus and that this coercion is their justification for civil disobedience. (More on this in chap. 7.) Operation Rescue considers itself an advocate for the baby, the defenseless pawn in this drama. Yet, the actions of Operation Rescue impose the same pawn status upon the expectant mother. This is the moral dilemma. To coerce the baby to death for the mother's convenience and comfort is morally wrong; to coerce the mother to have the baby for conservative Christians' convictions and conscience is legally wrong. The courts will never resolve this dilemma, because humans are not wise enough to judge between the value of two innocent lives—one innocent before God, the other innocent before the law of the land. Nor will the confrontational tactics of Operation Rescue resolve this dilemma.

The only possible solution is to turn to God and His commandments, where the mother would joyfully yield her rights to become the servant of her unborn child, and the church would become the servant of women in crisis pregnancies. This will not happen with the secular confrontational tactics of Operation Rescue. This can happen only with the prophetic preaching and practicing of God's word. It can happen if the church once again views children as gifts from God.

Without doubt, laws demanding abortion under certain circumstances are the step beyond laws allowing abortion on demand, but this has not yet happened. At present,

Christians must protest the wickedness of abortions—all abortions, for any reason—nevertheless they must not resort to obstructing the flow of traffic into abortion clinics until and unless laws are passed requiring abortions.

Another Civil Rights Movement?

Operation Rescue differs from the Civil Rights movement of the 1960s. So-called Jim Crow laws had created a de jure racial caste system in the American South. In the North, the system was often as oppressive, but it was de facto. The first step toward dismantling the Jim Crow laws occurred with the 1954 Supreme Court decision declaring public school segregation unconstitutional, but many Jim Crow laws were still in force in the 1960s. These laws not only allowed radical prejudice, they required it. People not only were allowed to separate themselves on a bus in Atlanta; they were required to do so. In response, men and women of conscience exercised their responsibility to disobey those laws, expecting the full penalty of the laws they broke. Their willingness to accept such punishment meekly, ultimately broke the power of these unjust and unconstitutional laws. If, however, the Jim Crow laws had only allowed the people to chose to separate themselves, the Civil Rights movement would have had the same ethical and legal problems confronting Operation Rescue.

One Issue

Operation Rescue is protesting laws that allow evil but not laws that mandate evil. Protesting those laws is right; obstructing others from functioning under those laws is wrong. Emotionalizing abortion by confusing the legal and moral issue and by ignoring this distinction has created its own problems. Abortion alone, among all of the legal yet immoral and ungodly activities in this country, is being singled out for civil disobedience.

Today, more Americans are harmed lethally by pornography than by abortion. Yet Operation Rescue is not obstructing the printing and distribution centers of this filth. Alcohol and tobacco destroy more adults than the complications of abortion; yet, there is no picketing of alcohol distributors and tobacco companies.

The world is not going to be impressed with a Christianity that picks and chooses its crusades on the basis of popularity, in this case, popular among those who oppose abortion. If Operation Rescue is right in physically obstructing those who seek abortions, they should also physically obstruct those who purchase pornography, alcohol, and tobacco. Tragically, many church members, including pastors and deacons, are enslaved by alcohol, pornography, drugs, and tobacco; therefore, these are not popular causes to picket.

Rebekah and Jacob Come to God's Rescue

God gave a divine promise to Rebekah that the "elder would serve the younger" (Gen. 25:23). Yet, Rebekah and Jacob did not trust God to fulfill His promise. They manipulated the circumstances and, through lying and deception, tried to make the promise come true (Gen. 27:5ff). What would have happened if Rebekah and Jacob had believed God rather than manipulating circumstances to fulfill God's promise? I believe that the greater glory would have been God's. We will not know in this life how God would have fulfilled His promise, but that He would have is as certain as His holy character.

God has promised that He will avenge all who shed innocent blood, and He has commanded us to leave vengeance in His hands. Yet, Operation Rescue has made it their responsibility to fulfill God's promise and to bring His judgment to the abortionists. The time will come when the cup of God's wrath against abortionists will be filled up. As certain as God's promise to Rebekah, God's judgment will fall upon America for despising His truth in legalizing wickedness. Christians in the pro-life movement should not repeat Rebekah's error. They should await God's fulfilling of His promised judgement.

Not a Good Samaritan

To employ lawlessness to uphold law, even lawlessness toward man's law under the guise of upholding God's law, ultimately destroys all law. Operation Rescue argues by analogy that what they do is like a person who, upon seeing a crime being committed, violates private property to stop the crime. Some in Operation Rescue would argue that even though abortion is not a crime, they are preventing a woman from committing a terrible act.

Arguments by analogy are fraught with potential abuse because unclear, imprecise, or inaccurate elements in the two circumstances can make the analogy invalid. Such is the case with Operation Rescue's argument that what they are doing is the same as any other "good Samaritan" rescuing the victim of a crime. The analogy fails on several counts.

1. A crime is defined by law. An act may be inherently immoral, ungodly, unethical and/or unrighteous, but to be unlawful and criminal it must be so defined by a statute of law. As offensive as it is to my Christian sensibilities, it is a fact of law that no crime occurs inside abortion clinics. The fact that abortionists and their assistants will be judged by God and will be punished by Him for their crimes against His truth does not change the fact that what they do is not criminal. When Operation Rescue trespasses to stop abortions, they commit a crime, but they are not stopping a crime. (Later, we shall see that this is what Paul commands Christians to avoid in Romans 12.) They are stopping a heinous, ungodly, wicked activity, but they are not stopping a crime. To emotionalize the issue is to confuse it. All

Christians should hate abortion, but unfortunately, in that we live in a democracy, that does not make it a crime.

2. Trespass is a crime. Trespassing is defined as the unlawful invasion of the person, property, or rights of another, committed with actual violence or violence implied by law. Yet, all trespass laws contain an element of intent, that is, an examination of the reason for which an individual unilaterally and without permission assumes the privilege of entering another person's property. For instance, if a house is on fire and a stranger breaks a window, enters the house, and rescues a child, he is neither actually nor technically in violation of trespass laws. However, if a building is on fire and in the confusion a person enters the building and steals a clock, he is guilty, among other things, of trespassing.

3. The Good Samaritan is accountable for the aid he renders. If one person, observing what is believed to be an act of violence being perpetrated against another person, crosses the boundaries of private property to rescue that person, he is neither actually nor technically guilty of trespass because of intent. If what is perceived to be a criminal act being carried out is in fact not, the good Samaritan may be liable for assault and battery and/or trespass. Good Samaritan laws generally hold a person harmless when rendering aid to a person in distress; however, good Samaritan laws do not protect a person against gross misjudgment or injury caused by stupidity.

An illustration of this would be a person who, seeing what he believes is an attack taking place, enters a private residence and forcibly disarms the presumed assailant only to discover that what he observed was a drama company practicing. If the actor is injured, the rescuer may be held criminally liable for a variety of offenses. Another case would be that of first-year medical students who observe a person collapsing in a public place. If they render usual first aid, they are within the bounds of acceptable practice. But if they take a knife and open the person's chest to do open heart massage like they saw on television the night before, they would be guilty of manslaughter. They would be held to a standard of common sense and sound judgment.

A police officer with probable cause can search private property, such as a motor vehicle, without a search warrant and discover the evidence of a crime. Lacking probable cause, the evidence he collects is inadmissible in a criminal prosecution. Perhaps the application of this principle may have gone beyond reason in our courts, but the principle is that of common sense and good judgment. It also applies to trespass laws to those who uphold the law.

4. A good Samaritan must summon police if time allows. The proper response to a crime is to allow the police to function. Unfortunately, Operation Rescue cannot report abortion clinics to the police because the clinics are not criminal. Not only does this prevent the police from interfering with the ungodly, immoral, unethical, unrighteous, but legal activities taking place in the clinic, it also prevents Operation Rescue from using the analogy of trespass in preventing a crime to justify their action. Abortion is a crime only when laws are enacted to make it a crime. Then Operation Rescue can expect the police to close down the abortion clinics and can hold them accountable for doing so.

If the time comes in this country when abortion is mandated, all of this changes. If the time comes when women are required, for whatever reason, to have an abortion, then men and women of conscience can and must obstruct abortion clinics. In that case, even though the law does not call what is being done a crime, law-abiding citizens must oppose the laws. Laws such as these are invalid and are criminal themselves because they go beyond allowing evil to require and/or coerce people to violate God's law.

Civil Obedience

Civil disobedience is either an attempt of a minority to impose its will upon the majority through coercion, intimidation, and/or force, or it is an attempt to liberate those who are being oppressed by the majority, which is determined by whether that which is being acted against merely allows what is opposed or requires it. Violent or illegal civil disobedience on the part of Christians is often the result of the misapplication of Christian doctrine initiated by the Social Gospel movement. There is no single illustration in the Scripture of violent civil disobedience, and most historical examples fail when examined by the life and character of Jesus. Secular social activism also is a result of the church's neglecting legitimate ministries.

Social activism will not solve the problems of society. Jesus said: "For ye have the poor with you always, and whensoever ye will ye may do them good: but me ye have not always" (Mark 14:7). This was Jesus' reply to the social activists who objected to Mary's anointing of His head with precious ointment. Jesus did not say that we would have the poor with us most of the time; He said that we would have them with us always.

Of course, we are still responsible to care for the poor among us. A brief reading of the prophets reminds us of that (Isaiah 58; Jeremiah 22). Unless it is imagined that these are Old Testament truths with no New Testament application, a quick reading of James 2:14–20 and 1 Timothy 6:17–18 will dispel such a myth.

God has a special love for the poor because the poor have a greater capacity for richer faith (James 2:5). It is the responsibility of the rich to care for the needs of the poor. The poor, in fact, are a kind of laboratory in which Christian faith is to be worked out. They are not guinea pigs, but they are part of God's design for the perfecting of

His people in preparation for eternity. This is not a misplaced noblesse oblige, but a genuine manifestation of the effect of faith in Christ, which is love.

Yet, even with our responsibility to care for the poor, all of the social programs in the world will never solve the problem of poverty. Jesus said that the poor would always be with us. His statement was both prophetic (telling the circumstances in which our salvation would be worked out) and practical (describing the way things really are). If this is true, why do we believe that social activism or its subcategory, civil disobedience, will eradicate abortion?

The prophets called for repentance, not a social program. They knew that only God could enable a person to repent, for repentance is a gift of God (2 Tim. 2:25–26). In the final analysis, social activism misplaces the focus from the church to the community, and God has no eternal purpose for the human community. That community's purpose will be fulfilled at the coming of Christ. However, the church is the Bride of Christ. She is appointed to be spotless and pure, which is her preparation for eternity.

The prophets of Israel addressed social evils only as they influenced or were adopted by God's covenant people. The prophets never imagined that they would sanctify the secular community. They understood that God required only that His people could be sanctified. Once again, this does not justify indifference toward social evils; it only shows that God has no eternal concerns for the world around the church. In the few instances where prophets like Jonah addressed the general, secular society, reformation was never suggested. Repentance was the only action they demanded to gain favor with God.

Christians must be socially responsible, which means we will care about human suffering and will attempt to relieve physical suffering. Christians, however, must not believe that human agencies will ultimately solve the fundamental problems of men and women. Those solutions require spiritual regeneration through God's intervention.

Jesus was not an activist. The only incident of activism by Jesus was His cleansing of the temple, but even this was not social activism. He drove the moneychangers out of the temple. There were all manner of social evils present in His day, yet He seemingly ignored them and focused on the eternal needs of man.

Jesus had compassion for the poor and the sick. He fed thousands and healed hundreds. Yet He did not found a hospital, a school, or a reform program. He founded the church that has the mission of ministering the grace of God to the physical and spiritual needs of the community around it. The solution to the church's abandonment of her responsibilities is not in creating social programs, but repentance.

Skeptics believe that Jesus was a product of His time and did not see the evil of slavery and other social ills of His day. Jesus recognized many evils in society, but His primary concern was to demonstrate God's ultimate concern for eternal matters. This is why Paul showed more concern for the eternal issues of the name of God and His doctrine than for the social circumstances of slaves and masters (1 Tim. 6:1–3).[1]

Subtly, Operation Rescue has assumed the world's agenda without knowing it by accepting the world's methodology of civil disobedience through social activism. The real concern should be for the name of God and His doctrine. While abortion is an abomination, the damnable thing was the rejection of God as the Creator that allowed abortion in America to begin with.

God's people have always lived as pilgrims and strangers in this world. God's focus has always been on the attitudes, motives, and thoughts of His people, that is, upon their personal holiness. Conduct and conversation, both of which are observed from the outside, are concerns, but conduct is clearly understood to be dependent upon the inner life (see Matthew 15). It is therefore the inner life that is of chief concern to God. (see 1 Sam. 16:7).

This is no flight from the real world to concentrate only on the inner life. It is, however, to say that the external practice of abortion by the secular community is no more grievous to God than the racism, bigotry, and social prejudice in the hearts of those in the church.

No society is strengthened by efforts to oppose wrong with efforts that undermine obedience to law, arguing that their minority view should take precedence over the majority opinion expressed in the law of the land. Operation Rescue's methods violate the spirit of Jesus Christ. Those methods displace God's spiritual and eternal focus to a secular and temporal focus. They turn Christian conviction into social activism and thus make crusaders out of Christians whom God called to preach the truth. For these and other reasons, I believe that Operation Rescue, passionate as it is, is operating outside of God's providence and is therefore subject not only to the judgment of man, but also to the judgment of God.

4

THE ROOTS
OF VIOLENCE

HOW DID THE PRO-LIFE movement come to encompass the acts of violence like those of Michael Griffin, Paul Hill, and those allegedly performed by John C. Salvi III? We must look to Operation Rescue for the answer to this question. Griffin, Hill, Salvi, and others have taken another step beyond Operation Rescue's not-so-subtle threat of violence-for-argument, and they have gone on to advocate violence-for-principle. These are the roots of violence in the pro-life movement.

Randall Terry

After becoming Christians, Randall Terry and his wife developed a deep commitment to unborn children.[1] They spent hours demonstrating and doing sidewalk counseling in front of abortion clinics. As their commitment to the unborn grew, so did their frustration. Out of that frustration grew a concern that they were not doing all they could or should. Terry explained, "The Lord started to speak to us about His law being higher than man's law. We began to wrestle with our responsibility to obey God's Word above and beyond our obedience to man's laws."[2] Terry and his wife determined that to obey God they had to oppose abortion effectively, whatever the means.

At this point, Terry appears to have crossed the boundary. He apparently became obsessed with a responsibility to be successful in saving babies at any cost. Terry justified using any available means by appealing to the higher-law principle: Christians must obey God, even when it means breaking the law of man.

Certainly Christians can appeal to God's higher law, but when? We must not allow the government to impose laws requiring us to violate God's law. Yet, others may object when Christians try to impose a law higher than the law of the land. Anarchy could result (1) when Christians try to impose on others the higher standard by which they have chosen to live and (2) when government tries to force Christians to live by the law of the land when it violates their consciences.

Generally, Christians can appeal to a higher law under the following circumstances:

- Christians voluntarily choose to live by a higher standard than the law requires.

- Authorities require an individual to violate his or her personal conscience.

- Authorities prejudicially and coercively apply laws against a group within the society, resulting in genocide, repression, or alienation as a goal of public policy.

Neither of these latter situations presently exist in the United States, and the first is the constitutional right of all citizens. Therefore, any appeal to a higher law to force another to accept a Christian view of a particular matter is invalid and ungodly.

One can only wonder what would have happened if Terry had continued to pursue the godly course that he and his wife had initially taken. One can only wonder what would have happened if his frustration with what he considered to be limited success had not distorted his vision.

Instead, Terry concluded that he should no longer say to abortion providers and women seeking abortions, "What you are doing is wrong, and you ought to stop it." Rather, he decided to say, "What you are doing is wrong, and *we* are going to stop it." It is in the substitution of the words *we are going to stop it* for *you ought to stop it* that the roots of violence in the pro-life movement were planted.[3] When that transition occurred, violence—whether the low-order violence of Operation Rescue or the high-order violence of Hill's "defensive action" and Trosch's "justifiable homicide" —was inevitable.

Once Terry crossed this line, there were no brakes, no deterrent to the rush toward violence. When Terry set upon this course of action, I believe he initiated the process that resulted in the worst excesses in the pro-life movement, excesses that led pro-life advocates to resort to terrorism.

Terrorism places the innocent at risk for the success of a terrorist agenda. Without realizing it, Operation Rescue started using these methods. Police officers had to remove the protesters from the abortuaries, placing those officers at risk. At that moment Terry's nonviolent movement turned violent. Demonstrators treated the police officers, who were legally constituted authorities, as adversaries, even though those police officers were not forcing anyone to do evil. That act revealed the fundamental flaw of Operation Rescue.

Terry began to defend violence more and more. He said, "Gradually, I saw that when man's laws and God's law conflict, the believer has a responsibility and an obligation to obey God rather than man."[4] He decided that because the law allowed men to choose conduct that contradicted God's law, the laws of men therefore contradicted God's law.

When do God's law and man's laws conflict? God's law and man's law are in conflict only when the law of man requires or forces a person to violate God's law. There is no biblical imperative for Christians imposing God's law upon another, either by the low-level force of Operation Rescue or by the high-level force of "defensive action" or "justifiable homicide." For the laws of men to be in conflict with the law of God, the laws of men must impose an obligation, with associated penalties for the failure to meet those obligations, which would cause men to neglect or to violate their commitment to God. Nowhere in the United States does that circumstance exist.

Terry described Operation Rescue in military terms and said, "During the spring of 1986, I realized that . . . we were losing the war." [5] Terry's talk about "war" and "losing on almost every front" in an activity that is going to have two highly motivated and emotional sides confronting one another is the dynamic that produces violence.

Terry's goal became "to win," so he had to improve his battle plan. Since when is the Christian's goal to win? In fact, when one determines that his principle goal is to win, he makes it impossible to follow Christian principles. For Christians, winning is a foregone conclusion, because God is sovereign and will be victorious. Until the final judgment, Christians must invite everyone to salvation as a primary goal of any contact, even to the point of Christians' suffering injustice in the world today.

Terry stepped closer toward violence when he said, "The pro-life movement was not creating the tension and upheaval necessary to produce political and social change." [6] He went on to claim, "Political change occurs after enough social tension and upheaval is created. We can save children and mothers today and ultimately end the American holocaust through nonviolent civil disobedience." [7]

Tension and *upheaval* are terms of force and conflict that almost always result in violence. In another 1989 statement, Terry said, " The anti-abortion movement [has] been 'too nice' during the 1980's. . . . We cry that abortion is murder, it's child-killing, and we carry a picket once or twice a year and write a few letters. . . . That's not an adequate response to murder. A logical response to murder is physical intervention on behalf of the victim." [8]

Here is the root of violence in the pro-life movement, and it is in a supposedly nonviolent movement. Adopting secular power politics does not honor God. Tension and upheaval are not methodologies that God employs in accomplishing His purposes.

As a foundation for his philosophy, Terry adopted a view of spirituality requiring social activism.[9] The Bible certainly holds believers responsible for the poor and the widows in their sphere of influence, but does the Word of God charge believers to "deliberately seek out the fatherless and the widow"? The Great Commission even addresses the responsibility of every believer to evangelize and disciple the lost in the context of their daily lives. A man may be called to go beyond his sphere of influence to serve or evangelize, but to suggest that a social activist's program must be initiated by the church goes beyond the command of Scripture. If every church took care of the widows and fatherless in its field of influence, all welfare programs could be dismantled. As is historically clear, no program can substitute for the failure of the church to fulfill its calling. The need is not for a program, but for a prophetic call for the church to return to her first love.

Prophet or Crusader?

Every Christian cause claims to carry on the work of the biblical prophets, but many are mere crusaders. What distinguishes a prophet from a crusader? When we read about the prophets in the Bible, what do we find?

- The prophet announced God's truth with God's authority.

- The prophet was sure judgment was coming if the people did not repent.

- The prophet endured the presence of wickedness because of his certainty of God's judgment.

- The prophet acknowledged that man's rebellion is God's problem.

- The prophet accepted his responsibility to point out the problem, but he recognized that it was God's responsibility to eliminate the problem.

- The prophet recognized that many good people were concerned about the particular problem he was addressing, but he also knew that God had not called all of them to focus their efforts in the same place.

- The prophet recognized that God allowed people to rebel against Him until the day of judgment.

- The prophet agonized over the evils of the day but knew that the people's refusal to repent was in no sense his failure.

The crusader, on the other hand, is characterized by::

- The crusader concentrates on only one issue.

- The crusader subordinates all other concerns to the one issue.

- The crusader works for the cause, which is his plan of action to resolve the issue.

- The crusader believes the problem could be solved if only people cared enough.

- The crusader thinks anyone not aggressively addressing this one issue is sinning against God.

- The crusader is concerned with one thing—success.

- The crusader believes that virtually any action is legitimate in solving the problem.

- The crusader believes he is personally responsible for solving the problem.

- The crusader considers anyone who disagrees with him on the issue as an enemy.

- The crusader considers individual liberty and individual responsibility negotiable if the problem can be solved.

- The crusader thinks the problem must be solved immediately.

The crusader and the prophet both have passion, but often the crusader's passion becomes his god, while the prophet never loses his personal passion for God. No issue ever becomes an all-consuming purpose for the prophet except the glory, majesty, and honor of God.

Was Jesus a prophet or a crusader? Jesus was a prophet, not a crusader. Jesus had no confidence in the political process. He was not indifferent to His responsibilities as a member of His community, but He did not employ earthly methods in an attempt to accomplish heavenly purposes. The resolution of all social problems and injustices will come from revival and ultimately from the return of Christ. We have already addressed Jesus' rejection of social activism as a means of advancing the Kingdom of God. Christians must carefully balance otherworldliness—heavenly mindedness—with this-world mindedness. It is possible to be "so heavenly minded as to be no earthly good," but it is also possible to be so this-world minded that one forgets that God's redemptive plan includes death and resurrection.

Is Randall Terry a prophet or a *crusader?* Terry is clearly a crusader. He has accepted personal responsibility for success in stopping abortion. He has adopted a spirituality that requires social activism. He has decided to create tension and to intimidate others into accepting his position on abortion. His preaching is not the prophet's admonition (What you are doing is wrong and you ought to stop it) but the crusader's threat (What you are doing is wrong, and I am going to stop it).

Love Requires Liberty

For Christians who believe in soul competency—the responsibility and capacity of every person to know God directly—the crusader mentality is particularly offensive in that it is willing to sacrifice liberty for solving *the* problem. When we sacrifice liberty, faith is no longer a function of love and becomes coercive. It does not honor God, even if we crusade for a good cause.

Terry is working against the terrible evil of abortion, but he has adopted authoritarian methods. A minority in a democratic republic cannot impose its deeply held religious convictions upon the majority outside of the legislative and judicial processes. The tragedy of virtually every modern tyrant has been the willingness to use any and all means, including force and violence, to expunge some real or imagined evil from society.

This is how the communists established their regime in Soviet Russia and the Nazis in Germany. No one would compare Terry and his passion for saving the lives of innocent babies with Stalin or Hitler, but their rationales for imposing their will upon their nations were the same. The fact that Terry rejected the overt coerciveness of violence does not negate this reality. Terry has rejected the actions of Michael Griffin and Paul Hill, but Operation Rescue's philosophy has logically led to Griffin and Hill's actions.[10]

Let's Put the Shoe on the Other Foot

Jehovah's Witnesses reject the use of blood and blood products to save human life. This is their deeply held religious conviction. Human lives are at stake, both if blood transfusions are withheld and sometimes even if they are given. Very few Christians agree with Jehovah's Witnesses about blood transfusions, and in certain instances, the state—through the courts—has ruled that it has sufficient interest in the welfare of dependent children of Jehovah's Witnesses to intervene and require that blood be given those children in crisis. To illustrate, let's examine two fictional cases based on the deeply held religious convictions of Jehovah's Witnesses.

Case 1: Reginald Terrell

Reginald Terrell is a Jehovah's Witness who is convinced the best way to stop the sin of blood transfusions is to block the entrance to hospital blood banks. He chains himself to the hospital door and prevents the blood bank from carrying out its functions.

What would Christians say about Terrell? "You can't impose your deeply held religious convictions upon others by force," or "It's a free country!"

Randall Terry might argue, "The circumstances are not the same. Lives are not being taken in the blood bank. In the abortion clinic, children are being killed." True, but Terrell would respond, "Lives are being taken. How many innocent children suffering from hemophilia have died of AIDS because of multiple blood transfusions?" Who could convince a Jehovah's Witness that this is not a judgment of God upon the ungodliness of blood transfusions? How many innocent women have died of chronic active hepatitis acquired from a blood transfusion during delivery of a baby? Terry might respond, "Not as many as from abortion!" The Jehovah's Witness would retort, "How great must the tragedy be before it is accepted as a tragedy?" Terry might declare, "But I don't believe that blood transfusions are wrong!" Exactly!

Case 2: John Q. Witness

The situation escalates when other Jehovah's Witnesses, frustrated because they are unable to stop this great evil, decide that they are sinning against God by being passive, arguing, if we have the right to forcifully prevent blood transfusions by blockading local blood banks, we have the responsibility to stop transfusions, they bomb the blood banks. When this doesn't work, several extremists, taking the logic of their fellows to its reasonable conclusion, murder a pathologist, as he prepares blood for transfusion. Everyone, except those caught up in the emotion of their opposition to blood transfusions, would understand how wrong these acts are. Everyone would understand that the murder of the pathologist was the logical result of the low-order violence of blockading blood banks.

This is exactly the sequence of events in the pro-life movement. Terry began protesting and preaching. Out of frustration over his limited success, he escalated his activities to include low-level and illegal violence against abortion clinics. Then others, sympathetic with his cause and frustrated at the failure even of Operation Rescue, bombed abortion clinics. Afterward, several extremists, taking the logic of Operation Rescue and the bombers to its conclusion, murdered abortion providers.

Secular Society's Schizophrenia

The state has generally held that parents do not have the right to allow their child to die because of deeply held religious convictions and at the same time allow parents to put their unborn children to death because of the absence of religious convictions about abortion. Here is the schizophrenia of the secular world. The world, which tells parents that they can take the life of their child in the womb and tells Christians that they cannot interfere with this right, tells Jehovah's Witnesses that they cannot make a decision that would result in the death of their child. Parents can kill their child because of the lack of religious convictions, but parents cannot allow their child to die in the face of religious convictions.

Christians who would support absolute religious liberty, even to the point of a child's life being sacrificed, find themselves in the schizophrenic position of objecting to the right of a parent to abort their child but supporting the right of a parent to cause the death of their child through neglect of a readily available medical treatment. Conversely, Christians who object to Jehovah's Witnesses allowing their child to die and who endorse the right of the state to intervene to stop harm to the child will of necessity invite scrutiny into how they apply their deeply held religious convictions both in the lives of their children and in the lives of others who do not accept their beliefs about abortion.

Legitimate Limit to Religious Liberty

Most Christians would argue that the state has a legitimate interest in the welfare of a child, which gives the state the right to say to parents, There is a limit to how far you can go in applying your deeply held religious convictions in the life of your child. Most Christians would argue that the limit of a parent's discretion with their child's life is reached when the parents' religious convictions would do permanent and/or irreparable harm to the child's life or welfare. This position is generally adopted on the basis of two principles.

First, the minor child cannot make valid volitional choices concerning his welfare, and the state therefore acts as his guardian until the child reaches legal majority. Second, the majority opinion in the nation rejects the position of Jehovah's Witnesses. Where their religious convictions irrevocably affect the life or welfare of the child, the state judges that it has an obligation to act on the child's behalf.

Having accepted this argument, however, how will Christians answer when the state declares, There is a limit to how far you can go in applying your deeply held religious convictions to the children of those who reject your beliefs concerning abortion? If Christians accept the state's legitimate interest in forbidding Jehovah's Witnesses from imposing their convictions upon their own children, how can Christians argue that they can and should, outside of legislation, be able to impose their convictions about abortion upon those who reject those beliefs?

Christians might argue that a child's life is at stake in abortion. The state would respond that religious freedom— the freedom to live by one's convictions—will be protected by the state, but while the state will protect one's right to live by those religious beliefs, it expects every citizen to recognize their right to require others to live by their religious beliefs is limited by the law of the land. Outside of the law of the land, no one can impose his religious convictions upon those who do not share those beliefs.

Christians might then argue, You refuse one group the right to allow a child to die because of its religious convictions, but you allow others to kill their babies in the womb, because they do not have religious convictions about abortion! In pointing this out, Christians would expose the schizophrenia mentioned above. Christians should preach and publicize the inconsistencies of the application of the law, not only in this instance, but in many other circumstances where the unborn child is dealt with as a real person with constitutional protection in one case and as a nonperson, lacking constitutional protection, in another.

The Law of the Land

The resolution to the abortion dilemma is simple: the law.

If Christians or Jehovah's Witnesses want others to obey their deeply held religious convictions about abortion or blood transfusion, let them have their beliefs adopted as the law of the land. If laws require or force any person to violate their deeply held religious convictions, then that person has the right to refuse to obey that law.

All men and women who have deeply held religious convictions should support the right of those who have different convictions to practice their faith within the legitimate limits discussed above. When a person of faith accepts any limitation upon the free exercise of deeply held religious convictions, as in the case of the children of a Jehovah's Witness, that person accepts limitations on the exercise of his own deeply held religious convictions.

We must apply this consistently. Christians cannot say, The state cannot force me to stop interfering with the right of another to have an abortion, but the state can force you to have a blood transfusion. No minority, whether Christians opposing abortion or Jehovah's Witnesses opposing blood transfusions, has the right to force its convictions upon anyone outside of the legislative processes of this democratic republic. Christians who would limit the right of Jehovah's Witnesses to impose their convictions upon their children when the life of the child is endangered must likewise accept the limitation of Christians' not having the right to impose their convictions about abortion upon others outside of legislation. Additionally, Christians must constantly remind the state of its inconsistency in regard to the unborn child, for, in reality, except when it is convenient to declare otherwise, almost everyone truly believes that the unborn child is a real person.

Is Operation Rescue a Peaceful Movement?

Operation Rescue claims to be a peaceful movement, but we must ask some questions.

- How can a peaceful movement compromise the constitutional rights of others?

- How can a peaceful movement cause police officers to be subjected to the potential of physical harm as they carry protesters? (According to Rom. 13:1–8, police officers are ministers of God.)

- How can a peaceful movement adopt a war strategy? This is not a "spiritual warfare" strategy, but a military-type campaign to force the will of a minority upon the majority.

- How can a peaceful movement communicate with military terminology? (Ammunition, front-line soldiers, medics, etc.)

- How can a peaceful Christian movement adopt the goal of "winning" rather than declaring the truth?

In the origins, plans, and practices of Operation Rescue, one can find the roots of pro-life violence in America. What the pro-life movement needs are men of principle who can recognize error in foes and in friends. The inability of the pro-life movement to be self-analytical and self-critical has resulted in the adoption of practices that contradict the principles of the Word of God. It also has resulted in participants uncritically accepting the methods of Operation Rescue, because they agree with its goals. This is an ethically immature and invalid process.

The violence in the pro-life movement came from the arguments and practices of Operation Rescue. Yet, the question remains, Where did Operation Rescue get its philosophy?

5

REVOLUTION AND CIVIL DISOBEDIENCE

I ONLY REGRET THAT I HAVE but one life to give for my country" is, for most Americans, a famous statement learned in a high-school history class studying the American Revolutionary War. For most Americans, revolution is a historical idea or, at worst, a current events study of emerging nations. For a few zealots in the anti-abortion movement, however, revolution is an option in their quest to stop abortion at any cost. In fact, advocates of violence against abortion providers speak of a doctrine of revolution.[1] They argue that "revolutionaries through the time of the Reformation [assumed] that society ought to be governed fundamentally by the law of God."[2] These modern revolutionaries have gone on to declare, "We support the principle of revolution and the goal of establishing or preserving a Christian government."[3]

In his chapter entitled, Time for Revolution?, Michael Bray declared, "Change will come, but not by the way Christian folk might like. Christians pray for revival, but revival involves high cost and radical change. . . . The desired change in the civil foundation of society may well come about through revolution."[4] Conservative Christians are often drawn to radicalism, because it gives the sense of opposing evil effectively. Unbound by biblical convictions, however, such passion could result in the same excesses seen in other countries where religious fundamentalism attempts to govern by theocracy.

Where in the Bible is there a doctrine of revolution? David never rebelled against Saul, even when Saul attempted to kill him. Paul did not counsel rebellion against the Roman government, even when he faced death. John did not foment rebellion, even when he was banished to Patmos. John the Baptist did not fight Herod's edict of death. Jesus Christ did not use force to deliver Himself or His friends.

Simply stated, there is no biblical doctrine of revolution. We will not find a biblical mandate or model for rebellion and revolution. Even in the Old Testament, there is no model of revolution.

In the wicked and oppressive Babylonian captivity, Daniel did not organize a rebellion against the king's edict about prayer. He quietly and personally obeyed God, accepting the consequences. His three friends—Hananiah, Mishael, and Azariah—did not rebel against the king. They simply and quietly refused to obey his evil edict. Their testimony is one of the most dramatic in the Scriptures. Charged to do evil, they said: "our God, whom we serve, is able to deliver us from the burning fiery furnace, and he will deliver us out of thine hand, O King. But if not, be it known unto thee, O king, that we will not serve thy gods, nor worship the golden image which thou hast set up" (Dan. 3:17–18). If these men had tried to force their beliefs upon the Babylonians, Christians would be without two of the most eloquent statements of true religious devotion in all of Scripture.

A Second American Revolution?

Operation Rescue founder, Randall Terry, justifies revolution by the actions of the clergy during the American

Revolution. He writes, "The Protestant clergy were the greatest force instigating and sustaining the revolution of the Thirteen Colonies' succession from England." Terry concludes, "There may be times when Christians will have to defy civil authority in order to remain true to God." [5]

As the leaders of the community, the clergy were involved in the Revolution, and there does come a time when Christians must defy civil authority to be faithful to God. The circumstances and the realities that made the American Revolution possible and necessary do not apply today, however.

The Declaration of Independence did appeal to higher law, but it was an appeal based upon the authority of the lower magistrate, not the right of any individual to impose his will forcefully upon another. The higher law on which the Declaration was based was the right of self-determination, the right of each individual to determine his own future without undue interference from others, and, therefore, the right of a group of people identified by geography and culture to determine their future. The Declaration of Independence, the Constitution, and the Bill of Rights were motivated by a desire to make men free to pursue their own destinies to the best of their abilities, without the coercive influence of government or of fellow citizens.

The Declaration and the Bill of Rights did not originate from a desire on the part of a minority to impose its deeply held religious convictions upon the majority or upon anyone. Yet, this is the very principle that pro-violence anti-abortionists have tried to abrogate. They wish to coerce others to comply with a standard of their choice, which is not required by the law of the land. As the Nazi abuse of power produced tyranny, this abuse, widely spread and employed by different groups with contradictory goals, would produce anarchy. No better illustration of this is needed than the insanity which took place in Oklahoma City April 19, 1995.

Unlike the French and Russian Revolutions, both of which led to terrible excesses, the American Revolution was not a revolt against indigenous leadership; it was a revolt against the imposition of rule by a foreign government. The Declaration of Independence was not an act of civil disobedience; it was a declaration of sovereignty by a nation in formation. Subsequently, England learned from this experience and allowed other colonial possessions peacefully to make the transition to self-rule.

The genius of the American experiment is that revolutionary ideas were placed into law, that made the government responsive to the people, both to the majority and to the minority. Therefore, the government expects its people to forswear violent upheaval, because the right of the majority to rule is defended, while the right of the minority to rail against the majority is held inviolable.

Against whom would Christians rebel today? What would be the object of a "new" American revolution? There is no illegitimate government in this country. There is no oppressive majority that has subverted the rights of the minority. There is no one who cannot speak, vote, write, or protest. Any rebellion in the United States today would be against the people of the land, not the government. Any revolution would be for the purpose of a minority to impose its beliefs upon the majority by force. That is not American, and that is especially not Christian.

All Americans—pro-life, anti-abortionist, pro-choice, and pro-abortion—can be thankful that the freedoms won in the American Revolution allow each American to follow his conscience under the law of the land. Each of these groups should be jealous for the protection of those rights, even and perhaps especially for those with whom they disagree.

It is in the protection of the rights of our adversaries, that we most clearly protect our own rights. When we are willing capriciously to amend and/or suspend the rights of the most insignificant and/or objectionable minority, we surrender our own rights.

The preaching of the truth does not violate the rights of anyone. The protesting of evil does not violate the rights of anyone. The attempt to force or intimidate someone into accepting God's law as his standard of conduct, however, violates his rights. As long as the rights of free speech, freedom of religion, freedom of the press, and freedom of assembly are held inviolable, the nation has the right to expect its citizens to eschew force or violence as methods to advance their personal cause. As long as these rights are maintained, there can be no valid appeal to a higher law as a pretext for revolution.

Dietrich Bonhoeffer and The Cost of Discipleship

The subtle violence of Operation Rescue is further demonstrated by Randall Terry's appeal to the life and work of Dietrich Bonhoeffer.[6] Many advocates of violence in the pro-life movement cite Bonhoeffer's example to justify their methods.

Bonhoeffer was a German Lutheran pastor and theologian who opposed Hitler and National Socialism. Bonhoeffer was imprisoned in Buchenwald, and at thirty-nine years of age, in a final purge by Hitler's order, was hanged on April 9, 1945, for his part in the June 1944 plot to assassinate Hitler.

In 1937, Bonhoeffer's best-known work, *The Cost of Discipleship*, was published. Concerning revolution and this book, Kenneth Earl Morris observed, "*The Cost of Discipleship* was so traditional in its Lutheran teaching on the duty of Christians to obey governmental authorities that, years later, Bonhoeffer referred his Nazi accusers to it as part of his defense against the charge of treason."[7] Morris argues that Bonhoeffer's political activity was motivated more by his family ties than by his theology, noting that his brother, Klaus, two brothers-in-law, and an uncle were executed for anti-Nazi activity.[8]

The advocates of violence in the pro-life movement argue that Bonhoeffer's participation in the plot to assassinate Hitler points to the right of Christians, appealing to higher law, to violate the laws of men to obey the laws of God. The truth is Bonhoeffer did not come to participate in the assassination plot out of a cavalier right to use force, but out of deep soul searching.[9] For Bonhoeffer, this was not a principle to be employed; it was a last resort. It must never be forgotten that Bonhoeffer's most quoted statement does not say, "When Christ bids a man, He bids him come and kill." Instead, he wrote, "Jesus Christ bids a man come and die."[10]

Although Bonhoeffer is a favorite source for support, pro-violence anti-abortionists quote him selectively. Bonhoeffer's writings do not support the use to which advocates of violence put his resistance to Hitler. He rejected violence and embraced intercession as the "doughtiest weapon in [Christians'] armory."[11] Bonhoeffer did not see force as a means to the end of carrying out the gospel mandate. He did not participate in the plot to assassinate Hitler to reform society or to impose his convictions upon society. He did so because a state of war legally existed and because the will for the continuance of that war was embodied in the person of one man.

There is no application of this illustration in today's America. In a system that is not coercive, in a nation where evil is only an option, not a requirement, Bonhoeffer found no justification for imposing his deeply held religious convictions upon anyone else. Even concerning slavery, Bonhoeffer found no excuse for revolt. He said, "Whether

Onesimus stays on as a slave or not, the whole relationship between master and slave has been radically changed. . . . This is how the Church invades the life of the world and conquers territory for Christ. . . . If a man is baptized as a slave, he has now as a slave . . . become a freedman of Christ . . . [and] acquired a freedom which no rebellion or revolution could have brought him."[12]

Revolution suggests a man has a need that God has not or cannot provide. Bonhoeffer argued that the work of Christ turned the world upside down and "wrought a liberation for freeman and slave alike." He concluded that a violent revolution "only obscure[d] that divine New Order which Jesus Christ has established . . . [for Paul] to renounce rebellion and revolution is the most appropriate way of expressing our conviction that the Christian hope is not set on this world, but on Christ and his kingdom."[13]

Bonhoeffer did not ignore the evils around him; neither did the apostle Paul. The revolution which Christians must precipitate, however, is not political or secular; it is the revolution of the gospel being lived through men and women loving their enemies and doing good to those who hate them. It is the revolution of looking upon all men and women as your equal, both in intrinsic value and in potential value to the kingdom of God. The temptation for the crusader is to become preoccupied with this world to the exclusion of the commitment to the principles of the kingdom of God. The need of the prophet is to let people know that their love for God must affect their relationships with all other men and women.

Change by Service or by Force?

Bonhoeffer rejected social reform as a goal for the church and argued that such reform was "the way of the world." He said, "The world exercises dominion with force and Christ and Christians by service."[14] Christ was not keen on reform, and neither was His disciple Bonhoeffer. It is impossible to advance the kingdom of God, Bonhoeffer argued, by employing the methods of the world. The world's method is force; Christ's method is service. It is difficult to determine how to serve the abortionist without facilitating his evil, but that is the challenge of the gospel. It is an easy thing to determine how to use force against the abortionist, but that is a corruption of the gospel.

It is difficult to imagine civil-disobedience advocates finding much comfort in these words. It is difficult to imagine Randall Terry, whose own statements on slavery are incorrect,[15] being comforted by Bonhoeffer's understanding of why the slave should remain in servitude. It is also difficult to imagine why Michael Bray, who advocates revolution, would find any kinship with Bonhoeffer who sees revolution as a betrayal of the gospel.

Just as the American Revolution and its appeal to the higher law of self-determination does not encourage or endorse civil disobedience, Bonhoeffer's act against Hitler does not encourage or endorse revolution. In participating in the plot to kill Hitler, Bonhoeffer attempted to eliminate the force behind the evil of Nazi Germany. He was not acting to overthrow the government of his land. He did not favor another party over the Social Democrats in Germany. He only opposed the tyranny of the Nazis.

Francis Schaeffer: A Christian Manifesto

Pro-violence anti-abortionists appeal directly to Bonhoeffer; indirectly, they are dependent upon Francis Schaeffer. While Bonhoeffer essentially rejected revolution against a legitimate government, Schaeffer suggested that a government could lose its legitimacy, making revolution a right and responsibility of Christians.

Schaeffer was a pastor in St. Louis, Missouri, when, in 1948, he moved to Switzerland and founded L'Abri Fellowship, an international study center and Christian community with branches in Switzerland, England, the Netherlands, Sweden, France, and the United States. Schaeffer wrote twenty-two books that were translated into twenty-five languages. Among his most widely read works are *The Great Evangelical Disaster* (1984), *True Spirituality* (1971), *What Ever Happened to the Human Race* (1979), *How Should We Then Live* (1975), and *Escape from Reason* (1974). He has been described by his publisher as "one of the most influential thinkers of the day."

Duty to Disobey

In *A Christian Manifesto,* Schaeffer alludes to a time when Christians should disobey the law and to a time when force would be required to obey God. He writes, "There does come a time when force, even physical force, is appropriate."[16] He never clearly detailed when that time might be, but he suggests that force was required because of the dwindling influence Christianity has in today's society, which he associates with pluralism.[17] Schaeffer introduces a rather contrived distinction between force and violence, which has been subsequently adopted by Michael Bray and Paul Hill.

Schaeffer defines *pluralism* as "each individual [can] grab according to the whim of personal preference. What you take is only a matter of personal choice, with one choice as valid as another . . . everything is acceptable. . . . There is no right or wrong; it is just a matter of your personal preference."[18] Pluralism was the problem, Schaeffer argues. What Christian has not been frustrated by the contempt in which his faith is held by a secular society? Is the answer a cultural hegemony produced by a modern inquisition that imposes an external appearance of

Christianity upon a nation without an internal change in the hearts of men?

Many would argue that personal preference and individual liberty are synonyms. While no one who believes in supernatural faith and in divine revelation believes that "one choice is as valid as another," in the context of secular society and before the laws of men, "one [legal] choice [is] as valid as another." Schaeffer's rejection of pluralism is biblically and ecclesiologically sound, but it is not politically or sociologically sound. The Christian and the church are governed by one standard; the citizen and the country are governed by another.

Schaeffer's Violent Disciples

To justify the civil disobedience of trespass, Randall Terry quoted Schaeffer's contention that the Roman government did not execute Christians, because they were exercising their faith, but because they were disobeying the civil authority.[19] This begs the question. Roman Christians did not employ civil disobedience to bring pressure on the Roman government. They were not trying to make someone else live by a higher standard. They were not even trying to stop the evil of feeding Christians to the lions. They simply and profoundly refused to submit to a law that required them to violate their personal conscience—to worship Caesar as god. Their refusal cost them their lives, but it did not bring dishonor to God. While what they did was disobedient, and while it could be called civil disobedience, to label it as such misses the point and leads to an invalid conclusion.

Like Schaeffer, Terry's reading and application of Scripture is flawed, because both have attempted to use the early Christians' refusal to submit to a coercive law as justification for modern Christians' attempting to force others to live by God's law. While Christians have the right and responsibility to work in the political arena to influence their country and their culture for Christ, they cannot do this by force or intimidation.

Schaeffer's influence in the pro-violence anti-abortion movement is further seen by his being quoted in Pat Robertson's foreword to Terry's book, *Operation Rescue.* Like Schaeffer, Robertson closely identifies Christianity with Western culture. It is my belief that God does not have a redemptive plan for countries or cultures. For Christians to identify Christianity with Western culture and/or the American church's prosperity is a mistake.

Schaeffer said, "We must work for reconstruction. . . . We should attempt to correct and rebuild society."[20] It is arguable whether there is a biblical imperative for culture regeneration or for rebuilding society, but all of the advocates of force in the pro-life movement have followed this line of reasoning. Christianity has had and should have a positive effect upon the community at large, but that is not the end that is envisioned by the gospel. The influence of Christians must be their faith, not the threat of force.

Advocates of violence claim, "The law [of God] is good and the institution of it in society has a salvific effect. It lifts society out of degradation."[21] (For more on this concept see chapter 10). The latter statement is true, but there is no gospel imperative for the redemption of society, and the influence of Christianity upon society has always derived from its positive influence, not a negative one. The influence of Christianity has also derived from the believers' obedience to governmental authority, from their commitment to family, from their rejection of drunkenness, from their responsibility to their obligations, etc. It has not occurred because they aggressively flaunt their "right" to rebel or their responsibility to reject the laws of the land, even though ultimately that right and responsibility does exist.

6

OBEYING GOD OR MAN?

WE MUST OBEY GOD rather than men." All advocates of violence and disobedience quote this, but have not examined the context of Peter's statement. Francis Schaeffer was one of the first conservative evangelicals to copy the liberation theologians' usage of Acts 5:29 in justifying disregard for the laws of men. He wrote, "It is not only the privilege but it is the duty of the Christian to disobey the government."[1] Influenced by Schaeffer, Randall Terry used Acts 5:29 to justify Operation Rescue.

A proper understanding of Acts 5:29 leads to a different conclusion. In Acts 4, Peter and John were ordered not to preach the gospel, "And they called them, and commanded them not to speak at all nor teach in the name of Jesus" (Acts 4:18). Peter and John responded by telling the Sanhedrin, "Whether it be right in the sight of God to hearken unto you more than unto God, judge ye. For we cannot but speak the things which we have seen and heard" (Acts 4:19–20). Peter and John did not challenge the right of the Sanhedrin to rule, nor did they demand their rights or call for revolution. They simply announced that their compulsion to speak of Christ derived from the internal pressure of a personal relationship with Christ.

In Acts 5, Peter and John were arrested again for preaching the gospel, not for civil disobedience, demonstrations, or protests. The Sanhedrin said, "Did not we straitly command you that ye should not teach in this name?" Peter answered, "We ought to obey God rather than men" (Acts 5:29). Like the Christians who later defied the imperial edict to worship Caesar, Peter and John refused to obey the instructions of men, when those instructions would have caused them to do evil; namely, cease to testify to the saving grace of Christ. They did not, however, try to force others to ignore the instructions of the Sanhedrin. They did not chain themselves to the temple and refuse to move until the edict was altered. They simply refused to do evil, and they suffered for it.

Peter Was Not an Activist

If there is any doubt that Peter's statement in Acts 5:29 was not given to establish a principle of civil disobedience to bring pressure on the government, a reading of 1 Peter will resolve that doubt. Peter was not an advocate of rebellion or revolution. He preached obedience to God, which sometimes would cause the believer to refuse to obey the laws of men, not as a principle of civil disobedience, but as a principle of conscience before God.

Peter balances the responsibility to obey God and the responsibility to obey the laws of men. Even when a Christian must disobey man's law in order to obey God— "For this is thankworthy, if a man for conscience toward God endure grief, suffering wrongfully" (1 Pet. 2:19)—he is not to do it in a way that brings dishonor to God—"As free, and not using your liberty for a cloak of maliciousness, but as the servants of God" (1 Pet. 2:16).

Most Christians would agree that there is a time when the laws of men must be disobeyed by Christians for conscience' sake. Most Christians would agree that there is a time for civil disobedience by Christians, but the circumstances in which it would be godly to disobey the law of the land must be clearly defined. Christians' disobedience to man's law is never civil disobedience, which has as its purpose the reforming of society. When Christians are called upon by conviction to disobey the laws of their land, they are simply desiring to be true to their confession of faith in Christ.

Schaefer not only suggested cultural pluralism was a basis for civil disobedience, he said that the use of tax money for evil purposes, particularly for the support of abortion, was a reason for civil disobedience.[2] Later, Schaeffer explicitly recommended tax protesting. He said, "In our day an illustration for the need of protest is tax money being used for abortion. . . . At some point protest could lead some Christian to refuse to pay some portion of their tax money."[3] Christians are greatly perplexed as to how to deal with paying taxes when evil is being done with their tax money. There is significant sympathy for withholding tax payments because of government's funding of abortion.

The reality is that tax money in the United States has always been used for purposes that are inconsistent with or in contradiction of the gospel message. Government subsidies of the tobacco industry and the federal purchasing and serving of alcohol are only two instances of this. When Christ instructed His disciples about taxes (Mark 12:14–17; Matt. 17:24–27), He did not address what Caesar did or did not do with the money—Caesar would answer to God for that. The disciples were taught that their responsibility to man's law did not conflict with their responsibility to God's law, unless or until, they were required to do evil.

Commands Contrary to Convictions

Schaeffer almost comes to the biblical position on when Christians should disobey the law, when he said we are not to be subject to the "man in that office who commands that which is contrary to the Bible."[4] This statement is correct. When the governing authority commands that we do evil— when the law coerces or requires us to do evil—Christians must disobey. Schaeffer claimed, "Any government that commands what contradicts God's Law abrogates its authority . . . at that point we have the right, and the duty, to disobey it."[5] He added, "It is time we consciously realize that when any office commands what is contrary to God's Law it abrogates its authority."[6] Again, these statements are correct. It is in "command[ing] what contradicts God's Law" and in "command[ing] what is contrary to God's Law" that government places itself in a position where Christians must disobey its decrees.

Schaeffer, however, does not follow up these statements. Instead, he suggests that Christians should disobey simply because the state allows that which is contrary to the Word of God. That is not true. The allowing of evil does not place the laws of men at opposition to the law of God. Unfortunately, Schaeffer's not building upon this foundation allowed his incomplete arguments to be used by those who would abuse his concepts.

Randall Terry's argument that pressure to stop abortion must be felt by the authorities—"they will see the light when they feel the heat"[7]—parrots Schaeffer's idea of pressure being brought against the government. Schaeffer had said, "In a fallen world, force in some form will always be necessary. . . . Christians must come to the children's defense. . . . State officials must know that we are serious about stopping abortion . . . the bottom line is that at a certain point there is not only the right, but the duty to disobey the state."[8] Yes. At a certain point there is the responsibility to say no to the state.

The question that remains unanswered in Schaeffer's writings is a clear, biblical statement of when and where that point is. While force will be required as an instrument of state policy, it is never an instrument of church policy. "Officials knowing that [Christians] are serious about stopping abortion" is not an excuse for terrorist tactics of violence and intimidation. That officials know how serious Christians are is not nearly as important as their knowing how serious God takes abortion. The former is possible by protest, the latter is possible only by the prophetic preaching of the truth.

Schaeffer's call to arms has been heeded by Terry, Hill, Griffin, Bray, and others. Unfortunately, his failure to define carefully when Christians should disobey the law leaves that judgment to each person. Also, Schaeffer's association of the Christian's obligation to disobey the law with societal reform turns Christian devotion into social activism. His advocacy of force by Christians led his disciples to violence.

Schaeffer further advanced the cause of violence by associating the loss of rights with the responsibility to rebel against the government. He said, "The Declaration of Independence states if [the people] find that their basic rights are being systematically attacked by the state, [they] have a duty to try to change that government, and if they cannot do so, to abolish it." [9] This statement leaves a great deal of latitude for misunderstanding.

Many rights of the Christian can be limited and/or eliminated before he is required by law to do evil. It is not the abridgment of one's rights that requires a Christian to disobey the law; it is the requirement of a Christian to violate his responsibility to God that demands he disobey the law of man. The suggestion that men and women should rebel against the government when their "rights" are being abridged—at best an extremely subjective and self-serving judgment—leaves the concept of revolution and rebellion to their emotions without the influence of conviction.

Schaeffer also makes the leap from the Christian's right and/or responsibility to disobey an evil law to his right or responsibility to overthrow the government, apparently by force. This last proposition was not established by Schaeffer, but it was inferred by Terry and Bray. Schaeffer almost glorifies revolution, arguing that it is a result of the gospel, saying, "In almost every place where the Reformation had success there was some form of civil disobedience or armed rebellion." [10] This statement will bear fruit in his disciples who will find a validation of their faith in their radicalism. This statement, however, unwittingly accepts the basic premises of the liberal distortion of the gospel known as liberation theology.

There is an element of truth to what Schaeffer has written, but applying this to the abortion crisis in America is inappropriate and dangerous. Because Schaeffer left so much unsaid, he allowed his writings to be co-opted by those less committed than himself to the gospel message. Once again, Schaeffer misapplies a historical event in trying to justify rebellion. He suggested, "If there is no place for civil disobedience, then the government has been put in the place of the Living God. . . . And that point is exactly where the early Christians performed their acts of civil disobedience even when it cost them their lives." [11]

Schaeffer's reading of history is accurate, but his application of the lesson of history is not. The early Christians were coerced into doing evil, therefore they refused. No Christian in America is forced to do evil, but should they ever be commanded or required to do evil, they should refuse. There is a place for civil disobedience, and the early Christians found it. One cannot find in the history lesson quoted by Schaeffer, however, an advocacy of force or violence in establishing the law of God as the law of the land.

All advocates of violence in the pro-life movement appeal to some definition of when a government compromises its legitimate authority and thus should be disobeyed by Christians. Unfortunately, none of them give a clear, definitive explanation, which leaves others to fill in the blanks as they go along. Schaeffer's work suffers from this same deficiency.

Three Problems in Schaeffer's Reasoning

Schaeffer fails to support his contention that while the Christian must and can legitimately disobey a law that requires him to do evil, such a law also makes it necessary for the Christian to overthrow the government. Three problems appear in *A Christian Manifesto:*

- The implication that there is a cultural imperative in the gospel, that is, a requirement for Christians to reform society. Holy Spirit revival will affect the community at large, but the church's attempt to affect the community at large through political activity will not produce that revival.

- The implication that the application of the gospel to a society will produce a certain form of government. It is true that liberty and justice are effects of the gospel, but there may be many forms of government that are capable of allowing these results. Western civilization is a product of the influence of the gospel, but it is doubtful that it is the end result of the gospel.

- The implication that biblical eschatology will be fulfilled wholly or partially by human political and social action. Christians should be involved in bringing food, shelter, and clothing to those without them, but they must never imagine that that is the end of the gospel.

These three implications do not come from the Bible. Accepting them leads to conclusions about influencing one's community or culture that are contrary to the gospel. Randall Terry, Paul Hill, Michael Griffin, Michael Hirsh, and Michael Bray have accepted these teachings of Schaeffer and have thus embraced a radical anti-abortionism that is unscriptural. Schaeffer's work formed the foundation for Terry's arguments on civil disobedience, and Schaeffer's work provided the bridge from Terry's position to that of Bray. Bray decided that the Supreme Court's decision's were not only immoral, as Schaeffer contented,[12] but illegal. He then advanced the assault from the low-level violence of clinic blockade and passive resistance, to the high-level violence of clinic bombings and ultimately to the justification of lethal attacks upon abortion providers.

SCRIPTURES USED BY THE ADVOCATES OF PRO-LIFE VIOLENCE

WE OUGHT TO OBEY GOD rather than men" (Acts 5:29). Absolutely, but as we have already seen, this affirmation by Peter is never an excuse for rebellion, revolution, or terrorism, and it is not an excuse for civil disobedience simply because the laws of men allow others to choose to do what we believe is evil. Just as the anti-abortion advocates of violence distort and misuse Acts 5:29, they distort and misuse other Scriptures.

Proverbs 24:11

"Rescue those who are unjustly sentenced to death; don't stand back and let them die" (TLB). This is Randall Terry's principal scriptural defense of Operation Rescue. No one proverb was intended by God to be used to justify something as contrary to Scripture as violence in opposing abortion, and it is particularly dangerous to develop radical action plans from paraphrases of the Scripture. There is no mandate in Proverbs 24:11–12 for Christians to impose their deeply held religious views upon others by coercion, intimidation, force, fear, or violence, each of which is a form of terrorism. The invitation to Christian commitment and/or the challenge to live one's life by biblical principles must be made without coercion or compulsion.

In the King James Version, Proverbs 24:11–12 states: "If thou forbear to deliver them that are drawn unto death, and those that are ready to be slain; If thou sayest, Behold we knew it not; doth not he that pondereth the heart consider it? and he that keepth thy soul, doth not he know it? and shall not he render to every man according to his works?" These verses allow for several interpretations and many applications, most of them spiritual.

They are a part of a very long section of proverbs attributed to Solomon. Proverbs are axiomatic statements of wisdom produced after truth has been processed through the calamities of one's life. Proverbs 10–19 contrasts wisdom and wickedness. Beginning in Proverbs 20, Solomon gives a variety of warnings and instructions to his son, and Proverbs 24 is a part of those warnings.

Solomon had learned through heartache that he was not king for his own pleasure. He had learned through calamity that even in his exalted position as temporal ruler over Israel, he must remember the welfare of his people. Proverbs 24:11–12 is given in the context of Solomon's warnings to his son to be attentive to the welfare of God's people. He was to rescue those who were being unjustly executed. As king, Solomon's son would have the power and authority to do this, and as the servant of the Lord he would be obligated to do it.

In "A Biblical Look At Operation Rescue," Robert L. Dean Jr. writes, "Perhaps the central passage used by rescuers is found in Proverbs 24:11. . . . It is clear . . . that the paraphrase . . . puts a slant on the verse that is more sympathetic to the aims of the rescuers." Dean's analysis affirms the general outline of the Proverbs offered above. He correctly concludes: "The direct application of the passage is to one in authority, not just anyone." There is no command in this passage for Christians to force their beliefs upon others; there is only the warning to those in authority not to violate the sanctity of human life.

Dean then addresses the application of these verses to the pro-life movement:

> To apply this verse to the plight of the unborn is at best a long stretch, at worst a misapplication. However, even if we do admit this as a legitimate application of the verse, all we get from it is an injunction to do whatever is in our power to help those being led away to death. There is no indication from this verse that violation of civil law is in view. The point of the passage is that those who are in a position to do something about a calamity are obligated to get involved, the extent of their involvement is not under consideration.[1]

Proverbs 24:17–22 supports Dean's conclusion. Solomon counsels his son not to let his life be controlled by what evil men do and not to join in revolutionary activities. This is consistent with the *Living Bible's* paraphrase of Proverbs 24:21–22: "My son, watch your step before the Lord and the king, and don't associate with radicals. For you will go down with them to sudden disaster, and who knows where it will end?" One wonders why Terry would not have read the entirety of Proverbs 24 in the *Living Bible?* Proverbs 24:11 is a command to be applied to the magistrate. If Proverbs 24:11–12 is unclear, Proverbs 24:21–22 is not.

The only application of Proverbs 24:11–12 in the pro-life movement is that one's voice must be raised against the evil of abortion. No prophet made God's people responsible for success; he called them to faithfulness. Ezekiel argued that if God's people—God's watchmen—saw the wicked about to die in his sin and did nothing, then the blood of the guilty would be upon their hands. The way to deliver oneself from guilt, Ezekiel said, was not to use violence or force to prevent the wicked from committing their evil, but to warn them (Ezek. 33:3–4, 9).

The way to deliverance for God's people is preaching the truth, not persecuting those who oppose the truth. There was no penalty upon the believers because they did not stop the wicked from doing evil; there was only a penalty if they failed to tell the wicked that what they were doing was evil.

Paul's sin in the death of Stephen was not that he did not use force to stop it; it was that he was consenting to it—Paul agreed with the death of Stephen. Acts 8:1 states: "And Saul was consenting unto his death." *Consenting* translates a Greek word meaning "to be pleased with, to approve together."[2] In Acts 22:20, Paul confesses, "And when the blood of thy martyr Stephen was shed, I also was standing by, and consenting unto his death." Paul did not lament not stopping Stephen's death, for he had no anxiety about Stephen's current state being superior to his former one. Paul lamented the fact that he did not protest or object to Stephen's death. Paul's responsibility was not to prevent Stephen's death, it was to announce the evil of it.

Proverbs 24:11 is not the dominant Scripture that impacts a Christian citizen's responsibility. Nor does the passage command a crusade against abortionists, pornographers, tobacconists, or prison wardens. What it commands is that God's people not be silent in the face of injustice. Jesus' life gives us an example of how to testify to the evil in the lives of others without resorting to force (John 7:7; 2 Tim. 4:3).

Exodus 22:2

"If the thief is caught while breaking in, and is struck so that he dies, there will be no bloodguiltness on his account" (NASB). The second Scripture most commonly employed in defense of violence in the pro-life movement is Exodus 22:2. This passage *does* permit the use of force for self-protection against someone who is breaking and entering, but it *does not* authorize vigilante justice. Christians still face the problem of applying this theocratic legislation in a democratic republic, except as it is adopted into the legal structure of that republic by the legislature.

While we might imagine for a moment that it would be wonderful to have a nation that was based on the Bible without the filter of majority vote and common law, we might be more cautious when we realize that it might not be our personal interpretation of the Word of God that was adopted. Notice the conditions surrounding Exodus 22:2.

- The criminal was a thief as defined by the law of the land, not just by common consent or common sense.

- The homeowner struck the thief. The construction of the phrase, "struck so that he dies," does not imply that the man was struck with the intent of killing him, only that he died as a result of having been struck while committing a crime. If a homeowner used the occasion of robbery as an excuse to take the life of another person, he would not be protected by Exodus 22:2. This theocratic legislation only covers the most extreme case because of the seriousness of the taking of another human being's life.

- The defender was a resident of the home or a passerby. This limitation would be implied by the fact that everyone who is climbing in a window at night is not a thief. Not every stranger climbing into a window at night is a thief. Without doubt, if someone mistook another for a thief and struck him so that he died, if the deceased were not a thief, the assailant would be guilty of manslaughter.

The context of Exodus 22 is domestic, that is, a resident of the home defending the family, not that of a vigilante committee patrolling the streets.

• The defender acted while the crime was being committed. An individual is not allowed to strike the man after the crime is completed or because he thinks he may go on to commit another crime. That is a matter for the authorities. Conveniently, Paul Hill ignored the limits governing the actions of Exodus 22:2, which are given in Exodus 22:3—"If the sun be risen upon him, there shall be blood shed for him." Even striking the thief, much less killing him, is allowed only if the crime takes place at night.

Matthew 7:12

"Therefore all things whatsoever ye would that men should do to you, do ye even so to them: for this is the law and the prophets." Perhaps the strangest use of Scripture by pro-violence anti-abortionists is their use of the Golden Rule. They argue that the Golden Rule not only justifies the taking of the life of another but actually requires it. Paul Hill explains, "The law of love teaches us that if deadly force is justified in protecting our own life, it is also justified in protecting our neighbor's life." [3]

It is an incredible and invalid leap from the proposition of doing good to others because we want others to be good to us, to then argue that we should kill someone because we would want others to kill anyone who is trying to kill us. The context of the Sermon on the Mount, and particularly the context of Matthew 7:1–12, contradicts Hill's use of the Golden Rule. The context of Matthew 7:12 is that of not harming others in that you would not want them to harm you. Any action taken against another must be examined in the light of Matthew 5:44–48, which would exclude Hill's bizarre interpretation of Matthew 7:12.

Jesus' affirmation in Matthew 7:12 does not leave us free to conclude that we are required to harm someone in defense of another, because we would want someone to use lethal force defending us. Extrapolating a positive commandment (doing good to others) to a negative situation (preventing the doing of evil to another) is fraught with problems.

While it is valid to say that we should protect the life of another when we come upon them while they are being assaulted, it is something else to say that we are responsible to go looking for people to rescue. It is an even greater distortion of the truth to say that we are required to kill someone to punish them for past evil, to restrain them from present evil, or to prevent them from future evil deeds.

If I am responsible for everyone without regard to my relationship to them, then where do I draw the line? Do I only draw the line with an emotional issue like abortion, or must I be involved in opposing oppression wherever and whenever it is found? Would I be less culpable if I refused to watch the news or read the paper and thus could claim ignorance of the crises in the world?

Is not the pro-violence anti-abortionist's position a subtle form of the liberal distortion of the gospel, namely, liberation theology? Is it not the case that I am to avoid committing evil in my own life and I am to oppose evil against my neighbor's life, but I am not obligated or allowed by God to form a task force to ferret out all evil in the world? The biblical concept of the near kinsman may give some understanding of how extensive our responsibility is and how aggressive we must be in exercising that responsibility.

In the Old Testament, not just anyone could step up and act as an avenger. Ruth's ancestral land could only be redeemed by her *goel,* her near kinsman, Boaz. Jeremiah had the right of redemption of his ancestral home at Anatoth.

To make every believer responsible for every societal evil presents tremendous ethical problems. We are, without question, our neighbor's keeper. While the young lawyer only wished to justify himself when he asked, "Who is my neighbor?" (Luke 10:29), in our society it is a legitimate question.

Exodus 1:17

"But the midwives feared God, and did not as the king of Egypt commanded them, but saved the men children alive." Paul Hill states: "The Bible also clearly allows us to take [whatever] action [is] necessary to protect innocent life if the government forbids it. In the first chapter of Exodus we see that the Hebrew midwives disobeyed Pharaoh's command to kill the newborn male Hebrew boys. This action was clearly approved by God."[4]

Hill's appeal to the Hebrew midwives is faulty for several reasons:

- No Christian should be involved in committing abortion. Christians whose jobs require them to perform abortions should change jobs or refuse to do their job.

- These midwives avoided the law to kill the Hebrew boys, but this does not justify killing an abortion provider. The midwives did not try to kill Pharaoh; they simply refused to obey his instruction. There is no evidence in the Scripture that the midwifes organized to influence other midwives; they only obeyed the law of their conscience themselves.

- Pharaoh's law required the midwives to do evil; American abortion law allows evil to be done, but does not compel it. The believer's response to the allowance for evil is different than the response to the command to do evil.

- The midwives responded gently to Pharaoh's terrible command. They didn't even tell Pharaoh that he was wrong.

Because the midwifes did not obey the government, Hill argues that it was right for Gunn's murderer not to obey the laws of the land in taking the doctor's life. The invalidity of this argument is obvious. The law of the land says that you cannot kill someone who is not committing a crime, but it allows you to kill someone when he commits a crime if your life or another's is in imminent danger. Even then, however, your intent must be to rescue yourself or another by the lowest level of force possible; your intent must not be to use the assault as an excuse to kill the assailant.

There is no compulsion of evil in America, and the midwifes did not try to kill anyone. There is no help for Hill's argument in Exodus 1, as there is no help in any passage of Scripture. It is interesting that the one whom Pharaoh sought to kill came to be reared in Pharaoh's household. Would Hill want the abortionist to have the responsibility for rearing the babies that pro-life activists rescued from death?

Matthew 21:12

"And Jesus went into the temple of God, and cast out all them that sold and bought in the temple, and overthrew the tables of the moneychangers, and the seats of them that sold doves." Most pro-violence anti-abortionists argue that Jesus favored force or violence. Paul Hill calls this "violent zeal." He writes, "God's approval of violent zeal is also seen in the New Testament example of Christ cleansing the temple of moneychangers. In Christ's example, the act was not only violent, but also an act of civil disobedience. Who could say whether His cleansing the temple helped stay God's hand of judgment on Jerusalem for a few more years?"

Overturning tables is much different from murdering a physician. Jesus' cleansing dealt with the covenant community.

He did not turn over the tax collectors' tables. He did not try to reorder society through the political process. He called the covenant people of God to consistent and consecrated living. He demanded that the church worship and obey God, but He did not set up a vigilante committee to make certain that the moneychangers did not return to the temple.

Jesus' act does not qualify as civil disobedience because He was not objecting to the activity of the moneychangers; He was objecting to where they were plying their trade and to their distortion of the true worship of God. Jesus' concern was eminently and preeminently spiritual, for His actions always foreshadowed the coming of the temple worship that would be in the hearts of men and women and boys and girls who are presently the temple in which God dwells.

Jesus' plans did not include the perfecting of society. "The poor," He said, "you will always have with you" (Mark 14:7). Evil, He said, would be increasing until the end of time. Passion for God, He said, would be distorted with passion for causes and for crusades. In the last days men will say, "Lo, here is Christ, or there; believe it not" (Matt. 24:23). Some of this deception will be in false revelations such as the best-selling book *Embraced by the Light*. Some will be in false prophets such as David Koresh. Some of this deception will be in false interpreters of the will of God, such as the advocates of violence in opposing abortion in America.

If "violent zeal" were God's design for His people, how would Hill explain Luke 9:51–56, discussed previously? Because of a personal insult, Elijah called God's judgment down upon a group of children. Jesus, however, declares that a new day has dawned. The patience of God, which is an expression of His mercy and grace, now gives men time to repent (Rom. 2:1–5). All of the laws of retaliation have been set aside, and the operative principle in the kingdom of God is forgiveness and long-suffering (Matt. 5:44–48).

Zeal for the Lord will now be manifested in personal obedience to His Word and the proclamation of that Word to others publicly. Zeal will involve holding up a high standard of holiness and righteousness. Zeal will be for the good of others and for the glory of God.

Christian zeal is not violent. It will not be manifested by forcing a confrontation that some hope will require God to declare His kingdom, as Judas Iscariot may have thought when he betrayed our Lord. Zeal will not be seen in cutting off the ears of those who reject and oppress Christ, as Peter did when Jesus was taken into custody. Zeal will not be seen in calling the wrath of God down on those who crucified Christ. Zeal will not involve harming others because they violate God's ways.

Zeal will be a passion to see the glory of God by seeing men and women repent of their sins. The only way for anyone to avoid the consequences of sin is to repent, not to kill. If pro-life activists want America to be saved from God's judgment, they must repent of the sorry state of the church and pray for God to pour out a spirit of revival upon America, for that is the only Godly way in which abortion will be stopped.

Luke 22:35–36

"And he said unto them, When I sent you without purse, and scrip, and shoes, lacked ye any thing? And they said, Nothing. Then said he unto them, But now, he that hath a purse, let him take it, and likewise his scrip: and he that hath no sword, let him sell his garment, and buy one." Reflecting on this, Michael Bray stated, "The account of Jesus commanding His disciples to take swords with them illumines both the continuity of the biblical teaching on legitimate force and the principle of role distinction . . . as the ministry of Christ was drawing to a close, Jesus recalled the former instructions (Luke 22:34); and then gave the apostles new instructions (Luke 22:36)."5 The idea of "role distinction" is that Christ's role as redeemer made His life unique and therefore not a pattern for His disciples after His death and resurrection.

Such an idea is strange. Why would Jesus live His life one way and then tell His disciples they were to live theirs in another? Both Peter and Paul, as did their Savior, prepared those whose lives they influenced for the inevitability of going on with Christ after the death of their leaders. Paul's greatest desire was that those whom he discipled would continue to obey God when he had left them (Phil. 2:12). He did not live one way before them and then tell them to live a different way when he was gone. Peter told the Christians of the Jewish Diaspora that they were to maintain the same pattern of life after his death as they had while he was with them (2 Pet. 1:12–15). Rather than being distinctive, the role of Jesus was demonstrative for all believers for all time.

Bray's distortion of the priorities of the gospel causes him to distort the application of the Word of God. There is absolutely no evidence that the disciples understood this as Jesus' meaning in Luke 22.6 When Jesus told Peter by what manner of death he would die in Luke 24, he didn't say, "Well, they won't do that to me, because I've got my trusty sword at my side." There is no evidence in the Book of Acts that Paul or anyone else raised a sword in their own defense. Paul could certainly have done that at Thessalonica if he had so understood the teaching of Christ (Acts 17:1ff).

This is not to deny that Christians can properly use force in some situations, but we must not use force to impose our faith upon another. What is denied is the use of force in a democratic republic to impose religious conviction against abortion upon a secular society. We can change the laws of the land. We can preach and prophesy, but we cannot and should not terrorize, intimidate, or coerce others to obey the truth. God does not do that, and we cannot and should not do it.

If "role distinction" is a valid hermeneutical principle, which explains why Christians are not to be gentle, humble, and submissive, as Christ was on earth—and I do not believe that it is—how does Bray deal with 1 Peter 2:21, Romans 15:7, James 5:10, 1 John 2:6, Revelation 12:11, and Hebrews 12:4? Many other biblical passages teach that the life of Jesus was normative for us and that Christ's kingdom is yet within us and not around us. His life shows us how to live our lives, and He died and rose again to empower us to live by the same principles and power that He did.

In every aspect of His life—obedience to the Father, dependence upon the Father, devotion to the Father, attitudes toward men, actions for men, desires for men, forgiveness of others, relinquishing of rights, and every other aspect of His incarnate life—Jesus lived, acted, and thought exactly as He expects us to do today. He lived the same Spirit-filled life that He desires for every believer today. The greater works that we will do include seeing the power of God work through sinful humanity in our lives, as that power worked through sinless humanity in Jesus' life. Bray's doctrine of role distinction verges on heresy.

In association with the concept of role distinction, Bray introduces the doctrine of progress. It is in this context that Bray argues that Jesus and the apostles did not teach all the doctrine that men would need, and that subsequent generations would need to supplement the Scriptures in dealing with social problems.[7] These supplements changed the way in which Christians should properly respond to society's problems, he contends.

Bray repeatedly argues that nothing changed from the Old Testament to the New. He adopts this as a hermeneutical principle to justify his advocacy of violence against those who are breaking God's laws. Now he claims that while nothing changed from the Old to the New Testaments, things did change within the New. Jesus initially told His disciples to be peaceable, but, Bray argues, He then gave them instructions to take up the sword. How can nothing change from the Old to the New and then radically change within the New? Bray's doctrine of progress is yet another distortion of Jesus' teachings.

In reality, the mission of the church never changes. It is simply to honor, glorify, and exalt the Lord Jesus Christ through pleasuring God with our worship, preparing the saints through training, and proclaiming the atonement by preaching and evangelism. Methods may change, but the mission is the same. Bray's confusion on this point allowed him to substitute the welfare of the unborn, rather than the worship of God, as the ultimate concern of the church.

The passing of time does confront the church with circumstances not faced by previous generations. Hit-and-run driving was not known in ancient times. Terrorist bombings such as in Oklahoma City and of aircraft were not known in Christ's time on earth. Yet the principles that gave direction and instruction to the Old Testament prophets and to the New Testament apostles, being eternal and universal because they were drawn from and based on the Word of God, which itself is eternal and universal, give clear direction and instruction to us today. There can be no "progress" (a nineteenth-century idea at best) in truth, because truth, while not static, is unchanging. There can be progress in our understanding of truth, there can be changing circumstances to which we apply truth, but truth does not change.

The Scriptures do not justify defensive action, role distinction, the doctrine of progress, or violent opposition to abortion. The conduct of the Lord was normative for all believers. As we examine the question of violence against abortion providers, it is legitimate to ask, What would Jesus do about abortion in America today?

8

REJECTING VIOLENCE

STEP OUTSIDE!" "My old man can whip your old man!" "Let's settle this like men!" These challenges are the stuff of jokes, movies, fiction, and adolescence. Everyone has heard them; few have ever taken them seriously. Men have not resolved their disputes by dueling and fistfighting since the American frontier disappeared. Yet, thirty-two people signed Paul Hill's declaration on defensive action. While this number may be small, other anti-abortionists are speaking out in support of some level of violence to solve the problem of abortion. These highly motivated and sincere Christians believe in and practice violence against abortion clinics and/or abortion providers.

Christians who reject violence as a method in opposing abortion are placed in a difficult position by several convictions:

- The child in the mother's womb is a human baby from conception.

- The child in the mother's womb is innocent and without moral guilt.

- Taking the child's life in the womb is a sin against God and man.

All pro-life Christians share these convictions, therefore, the pro-violence anti-abortionists ask, Why should Christians object to any act that protects the child's life, even a violent act? Why do I argue that it is wrong for Christians, at the present time, physically, forcefully, and/or violently to interfere with those who are seeking abortions? The reality is, if we cannot answer these questions, we cannot stop the killing of abortion providers. If we cannot answers these questions, we cannot get back to a righteous response to the evil of abortion.

The Innocent Always Suffer

In a world that is inherently self-destructive and rebellious toward God's law, the innocent suffer because of the choices of the guilty. This is a grief to good men and women, but it is one of the realities of a fallen world. Innocent children contract AIDS because of contaminated blood supplies. Innocent children become addicted to drugs because of the mother's habits during pregnancy. Innocent families are killed because of drunken drivers. Innocent bystanders are injured by accidents caused by high-speed chases, as police attempt to apprehend felons.

No matter how much he desires, man cannot suspend this reality. To guarantee that the innocent will not suffer, there would have to be an autocratic authority that dictates choices with no right of appeal. To be absolutely consistent, such power would have to be invested in one individual, and there is only one whose wisdom, compassion, mercy, knowledge, and power are such that He can be trusted to exercise this power, and that is God.

Men can attempt to minimize the suffering of the innocent through laws, but because man's laws are imperfect and because men are unwilling to obey those laws voluntarily, innocent people will continue to suffer at the hands of the wicked. In addition, God Himself does not force men and women to obey Him, even when their children will be negatively affected. The sinful choices of parents have always affected their children. Exodus 20:5 states, "Thou shalt not bow down thyself to them, nor serve them; For I the LORD thy God am a jealous God, visiting the iniquity of the fathers upon the children unto the third and fourth generation of them that hate me." The Bible says of Ahazaiah, "He also walked in the ways of the house of Ahab: for his mother was his counselor to do wickedly. Wherefore he did evil in the sight of the LORD like the house of Ahab; for they were his counselors after the death of his father to his destruction" (2 Chron. 22:3–4). God does not punish children for the sins of their parents (Deut. 24:16), but the weaknesses and wickedness of parents will negatively affect their children.

This principle goes back to Cain and Abel. While Cain was a murderer, he was so because he was the son of his father, Adam. If God had chosen, He could have destroyed Adam when he manifested a tendency for rebellion. God, however, allowed Adam to pass that weakness to his children. God did not kill Adam because of the potential negative impact of Adam's character upon his children.

If God will not coerce men to obey Him, so unborn children, grandchildren, and great-grandchildren will not be harmed, we are hard pressed to justify our coercing others to obey God in an attempt to prevent their unborn children from being harmed by their wickedness and/or weaknesses. Therefore, Christians cannot demand that nonbelievers comply with a law higher than that of the land, even the law of God, simply because, if they do not, their unborn children will suffer.

Limits of Liberty

Religious freedom has legitimate limits. Jehovah's Witnesses can be required to allow their children's lives to be saved with blood transfusions. Pro-life Christians can be required to allow others to exercise their constitutional options under the law without fear of attack. Christians must accept this limit on their religious freedom. This is not a compromise, rather, it places Christians in a stronger position to reject the excesses of the secularization of society as they reject the excesses of forcing others to live by Christians' religious beliefs.

Jesus' disciples once asked Him to call fire down from heaven against unbelievers. The disciples did not yet understand true faith, and they wanted to force others to yield to Christ. Of course, Jesus rejected this violent solution (Luke 9:51–56). Instead, He invites people an opportunity to serve Him, which requires them to be given the time and freedom to make their own choices.

Liberalism and Legalism

Disciples today are caught between liberalism and legalism. Liberalism makes relative, things that are absolute, and legalism makes absolute, things that are relative. Liberals try to justify abortion; legalists try to impose Christian values about abortion upon others by force or coercion. Jesus rejected both. He taught His disciples to preach, not to persecute. He taught them to follow Him themselves, not to force others to follow. He taught them to believe themselves, not to berate others who do not believe.

The Bible also declares that God's goodness delays His judgment (Rom. 2:1–4). No group is under a greater restraint not to judge others than Christians.[1] The ultimate manifestation of the judging of another, and of one man declaring that he knows God's ultimate purpose for another, is the act of premeditated murder. Christians should warn others that what they are doing is wrong. They cannot, however, consign anyone to hell or determine God's final plan for another person. All who worship Jesus Christ as Lord, Savior, and Master must therefore reject acts of violence.

God is merciful and delays His judgment to give men and women the opportunity to repent, but innocent people are hurt during this delay. This does not give Christians the right to arrogate to themselves what God has reserved for Himself, that is, judging the value of a man's life and determining when that life should end. Christians' enthusiasm for the protection of those whom they judge as innocent does not allow them to execute premature judgment upon those whom they judge as guilty.

Martin Luther commented on a man presuming to judge others. In regard to capital punishment, he said, "a judge can say, when by virtue of his office he sentences the evil doer unto death, that he serves God thereby. . . . We must make a distinction, however, for it is vastly different when a person punishes who has the office to punish, and when one punishes who has not this office."[2] Luther rejected the right or responsibility of individual Christians to impose their judgments upon others. He particularly rejected the right of an individual taking the life of another violently or forcefully, because the person had violated God's law. This does not reject the right of duly authorized authorities to impose the death penalty. It does, however, reject any individual as being so authorized.

In dealing with Romans 12:16 and 21, Luther wrote, "In forbidding us to return blow for blow and to resort to vengeance, the apostle implied that our enjoyment of peace depends on our quiet endurance of others' disturbance . . . he intimidates us from usurping the office of God, to Whom Alone belong vengeance and retribution. . . . It is not Christian-like to injure [our enemies]; rather, we should extend favors."[3] Luther rejected Christians taking the law of God into their own hands. He suggested that the greater terror—the terror of the judgment of God—

awaited those who had not been judged by their fellow man. Man cannot usurp the office of God, Luther declared. Only God can determine when a man's life is over. "Defensive action," like "assisted suicide," usurps the office of God, and must be rejected by Christians.

Is Abortion Murder?

The law of the land distinguishes between killing a child who has already been born and terminating a pregnancy, i.e., killing a child in the womb. There is no biblical or theological distinction between the born and the unborn child, but we live in a democratic republic, not a theocracy or a biblical republic. Christians are subject to the laws of the land, until or unless, those laws require Christians to violate their consciences and/or to do evil.

Abortion is an absolute evil. No argument against violence in the pro-life movement provides any comfort for those seeking or performing an abortion. Nor should Christians passively acquiesce to the legality of abortion in America. Yet a Christian response to genocide and/or the murder of a born child would be different from the Christian response to abortion. The legitimate and necessary Christian response to any law allowing parents to kill their already-born child would be different than our response to the law allowing abortion.

God will judge those who take the life of unborn children; however, in a democratic republic, such judgment must be left to God at the end of time. Yet, Christians would have a different response to the legalization of the killing of a born child than to the legalization of the killing of an unborn child, and, even that response would not justify premeditated murder, only the refusal to participate in such and the interjection of oneself between the one being killed and the killer.

Even though the unborn child has not volunteered for abortion and, in the sight of God, the unborn child has absolute value, Christians cannot coerce mothers contemplating abortion to accept a higher standard than that required by law. If the laws of the land are changed, however, Christians could expect the authorities to enforce those laws that require a mother to protect her child. If the laws of the land are changed so that a woman is forced to have an abortion, Christians should reject those laws and refuse to obey them.

Jesus Christ Connected the Dots in the Law

Pro-violence anti-abortionists attempt to apply Old Testament laws to a democratic republic. They ignored Paul's teaching on the relationship of the Old Testament to the New. Paul declared that the Old Testament law was "briefly comprehended in . . . Thou shalt love thy neighbour as thyself. Love worketh no ill to his neighbor: therefore love is the fulfilling of the law" (Rom. 13:9–10). Commenting on this passage, Martin Luther observed, "The Law had to yield for the time being, had to become invalid, when David suffered hunger. . . . Yield, therefore thou Law. Prevent not the accomplishment of this good. The Ten Commandments forbid doing evil to our neighbor." [4]

The Lord Jesus did not set aside God's law; He filled it with meaning. As stakes and planks lay out the foundation of a building, revealing its form, so God's law outlined the form of His will for men. As the concrete, framing material, walls, roof, and plumbing give further definition to the building beyond the form, so Christ gave definition to the will and way of God. He did not invalidate God's law; He showed us what the law had always meant.

Jesus did not redraw the dimensions of God's law; He simply connected the dots so that we could see what the application of the law always should have looked like. He showed us that the law was a training ground to teach us to live before God in a holy way. The law also was God's method of teaching men of their need for mercy and grace, as they were unable to fulfill the requirements of the law.

The law of God has not been annulled, but neither can it be unilaterally applied to a society governed by a representative legislature. The law is still valid, it has not been replaced, but Jesus revealed the true understanding of the law in the Sermon on the Mount. It is impossible, however, to apply the Old Testament law to a democratic republic except as it is filtered through the laws of the land.

Texas criminal law includes provisions from Exodus 22:2–3. If a person illegally enters your home at night, you will be held innocent if you harm him, resulting in his death. No questions will be asked as to whether you feared for your life. If the illegal entry takes place in the daylight, however, you must prove that your life was at risk if the person dies.

This is exactly the provision of Exodus 22:2. Nevertheless, the Scripture does not provide for, and Texas law does not allow, vigilante action against those whom we imagine are committing a crime against the law of God. And, the Scripture does not allow Christians to gather where they believe an infraction of the law of God will take place in order to prevent the infraction with force or violence. Nowhere does the Scripture allow a Christian intentionally to take the life of another as an act of self-defense or of the defense of another.

Theocracy Today

Michael Bray applies the Old Testament directly to modern situations, but modifies the New Testament message. He assures us that "Jesus . . . and the apostles . . . did not supply us with all the doctrine which we would need to handle all issues through the ages." [5] Where the Bible seems to support his argument—that is, in his direct and literal application of Old Testament law to today's society—Bray shows a high regard for Scripture, even if his hermeneutic is defective. Yet, where the Bible is silent or does not support his argument, he hesitates. He argues that "though the canon is closed, revelation continues." [6] It cannot be both ways, either the Bible is sufficient or it is not.

It is dangerous for religious leaders to endorse secular leaders without holding them accountable for their behavior. Bosnian Serb leader Radovan Karadzic,[7] who is principally associated with ethnic cleansing, was honored by the Greek Orthodox Church as a member of the nine-hundred-year-old Knights' Order of the First Rank of Saint Dionysius of Xanthe for his "contribution to the peace of the world." With this honor, the church encouraged him to wield the sword in a "holy" war. Endorsed by religious convictions, the passions and cruelty of men know no bounds.

The horror of members of one faith murdering members of another is the result of man's misguided attempt to impose his religious beliefs on another. The leadership of a theocracy is not subject to the checks and balances of accountability, as is the leadership of a democratic republic. Christians must not relinquish their responsibility for righteousness by embracing political activity or civil disobedience, simply because it accomplishes a goal with which they agree.

Will Theocracy Relieve Oppression?

Even biblical theocracy did not abolish oppression. The people of Israel asked Rehoboam to ease the burden Solomon had placed on them (2 Kings 10:4). Yes, oppressive governments violate the Law of God, but oppression also results because leaders reject their accountability to God.

> The United States governmental system affirms the accountability of the individual, freedom of choice, and responsibility to the community. At these points, at least, the United States operates under the spirit of the Law of God, even though many actively oppose that circumstance, and even though abortion on demand demonstrates how indifferent men are to the coming judgment.

Only God can found a theocracy. Otherwise, the so-called theocracy is really only despotism. Man's yearning for the rule of God on earth must be satisfied by God's rule in a man's heart. Well-intentioned, but misguided, people may try to force others to obey God and to love Him, but the so-called theocracies produced are really the ultimate expression of humanism. Such leaders exalt themselves to the throne of God, determining that any means justifies the end of their concept of the law of God being imposed upon others.

Bray proposes the founding of a Christian theocracy in the United States. He said, "We seek to erect a Christian constitutional republic . . . the state may not rule the Christian churches, though it must prohibit non-Christian public worship, if it is to maintain a just [that is, Christian] society." [8] Every modern experiment with theocracy has been a disaster—Jim Jones in Guyana, Joseph Smith in Utah. Pro-violence anti-abortionists may appear noble because they want to save unborn babies, but when their goal is carefully scrutinized it is actually no different from any other demagogue who has attempted to force his will upon others by violence.

All pro-life advocates would like to stop abortion now and protect the innocent children being killed by abortion, but these desires cannot be allowed to overcome the

Christian pro-life advocates' commitment to righteous ways. Christians cannot attempt to impose a pax Christiana upon the United States through force and violence under the guise of "obeying God rather than men." Nor can Christians attempt to bring the kingdom of God to earth through force and violence, as long as God patiently waits for His own judgment of evil.

9

Is Abortion
a New Holocaust?

Fire! fire!" so sounds the alarm as the one who raises the cry races out of the building, leading those who follow in their rush to safety. When lives are saved, the one who raised the alarm is a hero. However, if there is no fire, the "leader" could be arrested for raising a false alarm, and if there were only a cigarette burning on the floor, the leader would not be heralded as a hero, but ridiculed for misrepresenting the danger.

Leaders of violent anti-abortion activities have mobilized activists by emotionalizing the debate. Responsible leaders mobilize their followers without resorting to inflammatory language. A person is not a leader simply because others follow him when he runs out of a public assembly shouting, "Fire, Fire!"

Pro-life leaders have been shouting "Holocaust! Genocide!" which is as irresponsible as it is invalid. Remember, one's convictions should not require distortion in order to sustain commitment, and one's convictions seldom lead to violence, whereas emotionalism almost always leads to violence.

Here is a sample of Michael Bray's rhetoric. "The analogy between Hitler's death camps and modern abortuaries is . . . appropriate."[1] "Would-be allies of the unborn stand revealed as hypocrites when they equate abortion with the Nazi Holocaust but recoil at the use of the same measures that put an end to Hitler's."[2] If abortion in America is a Nazi-like holocaust, the same measures used against the Nazis would justly be used against abortionists, but if abortion in America is not a Nazi-like holocaust, Christians cannot use those measures justly.

What Is a Holocaust?

Holocaust is an Old Testament sacrificial term that has been applied to the systematic extermination of European Jews by Nazi Germany in World War II in which more than six million Jews were murdered. Nicholas de Lange explains, "The very term . . . indicates a recognition that this was something new, deserving a new name . . . 'holocaust,' . . . had not been preempted by any earlier historical event."[3] Having been "preempted" by the insanity of Nazism and the so-called final solution, the term should not and cannot legitimately be used to describe abortion in America.

The Jewish Holocaust

In the 1950's [*holocaust*] came to be applied primarily to the destruction of the Jews of Europe under the Nazi regime. . . . The use of . . . *sho'ah* to denote the destruction of Jews in Europe . . . appeared for the first time in the booklet *Sho'at Yehudei Polin* (the Holocaust of the Jews of Poland), published by the United Aid Committee for the Jews of Poland, in Jerusalem in 1940. . . . Up to the spring of 1942, however, the term was rarely used. . . . It was still far from being in general use, even after the

November 1942, declaration of the Jewish
Agency that a *sho'ah* was taking place.

ISRAEL GUTMAN, ED.,
ENCYCLOPEDIA OF THE HOLOCAUST
(NEW YORK: MACMILLAN PUB. CO., 1990), 681.

Judith Miller objects to the use of words that have
come to mean one thing in an attempt to form a bridge to
something else. She notes, "The word Holocaust . . . is a
palatable way of alluding to man's descent into almost inde-
scribable cruelty. . . . the sloppy use of Holocaust language to evoke the imagery of Nazi terror for
noncomparable situations has contributed, often inadvertently, to the relativization of the Jewish genocide.
Imprecise language is a culprit in many cultures. . . .
Abstraction is memory's most ardent enemy. It kills because
it encourages distance, and often indifference." [4] The use of
the term *holocaust* for abortion in America encourages distance and indifference among those who are marginal in
their opposition to abortion. Intuitively, they know that the
term is used inappropriately, and they thereby become more
complacent in their attitude toward abortion.

To use the term *holocaust* for any event other than the
systematic destruction of six million Jews trivializes the
tragedy of European Jewry. Pro-life Christians should find
their own term to describe the horror and tragedy of abortion on demand without the confusing images of Nazi
storm troopers and gas chambers.[5] Pro-life advocates
should also find a term to describe the horror of abortion
that provides a moral incentive for how abortion in
America should be righteously opposed.

Confusing the Issue

Argument by analogy fails if the circumstances between the

examples used and the applications made are not analogous. While there are a few similarities, there are significant differences between Nazi Germany and the United States in the 1990s. Several of those differences are:

- No government agents coerce private citizens to do evil.

- No one is required to perform an abortion to maintain a job.

- No one is required to work in an abortion clinic.

- There is no officially sanctioned public policy to encourage abortion.

- No one is required to have an abortion, not even the criminally insane.

- There are no government-maintained abortion clinics.

- Even *Roe v. Wade* only established the "right" of a woman to choose an abortion; no necessity is placed upon the government or private sectors to provide an abortion.

As objectionable as abortion is, it is nonetheless the case that there is a closer analogy between those who would murder abortionists and Hitler, than between those who provide abortions and Hitler. The capricious taking of another's life as an act of political policy is evil. Whether that act was perpetrated by Nazis who desired to see their vision of the future succeed, or by pro-violence anti-abortionists who desire to see their vision of society succeed, the moral value of the act is the same.

The confusion of abortion in America with the Nazi Holocaust in Europe:

- Diminishes the horror of the Holocaust

- Diminishes Christians' effectiveness in opposing abortion

- Confuses the ongoing ethical debate in America

- Makes violence in the pro-life movement much more likely by emotionalizing the issue

- Allows abortionists to focus on the sins of the church, rather than face their own sin

- Is an act of slothfulness as anti-abortionists neglect the exercise of establishing a term that properly describes abortion-on-demand in America

Nuremberg and Abortion in America

Some argue that the trials of Nazis at Nuremberg provide a model for the indictment both of those who participate in abortion in America and those who reject violence in opposing the evil of abortion. Objectively, the issues raised by the Nuremberg trials do not apply to abortion on demand in the United States presently.[6]

On August 8, 1945, the United States, France, Great Britain, and the Soviet Union signed the Charter of the International Military Tribunal. The charter argued that the only way to do away with tyranny and coercion by a government against its own people was through making government officials answerable to the international community and to the moral law that is common to all. For purposes of comparing any circumstance to the Nuremberg Trials, this is a pivotal statement.

At Nuremberg, *law* referred to human law as codified in civilized nations all over the world. In some respects this was an appeal to "higher" law, because it established that the laws of an individual nation are subject to review by the international community in regard to certain crimes. Those crimes were defined in the indictment as crimes against the peace, crimes against the laws and customs of war, and crimes against humanity.

Many defendants attempted to excuse themselves by arguing that they were simply complying with the laws of their land, which is called "legal positivism," that is, a person will be judged by the laws of his nation at the time he commits an act. If a person can demonstrate, this argument states, that he was actually obeying a law of his land, he can then be excused for participating in horrible crimes. Some who have opposed Operation Rescue and/or the more radical pro-violence anti-abortionists, such as Hill and Bray, have been accused of "legal positivism,"[7] that is, obeying the laws of the United States that allow crimes against humanity—namely, abortion.

The reality is that obedience to no law excuses one from the personal choice to do evil. Nevertheless, it is not evil to oppose violence against the law when that law only allows others to make a personal choice to do that which my deeply held religious convictions determine is evil. The decision to obey the law when evil is simply allowed by the society does not make one guilty of war crimes.

The London Charter disallowed the defense of "legal positivism." The charter empowered the Nuremberg tribunal to prosecute German officials for crimes against humanity "whether or not [their actions were] in violation of [the] domestic law of the country." In his review of the Nuremberg trials, Michael Hirsh observed, "The accused could not absolve themselves by cloaking themselves or their actions with German positive law."[8] The question for us is, Do these considerations *allow* Christians, indeed, do these considerations *require* Christians to oppose abortion forcefully and violently at this time in the United States?

The eighth of the twelve trials at Nuremberg is known as the *RuSHA* case.[9] The indictment charged that the Main Race and Resettlement Office designed and initiated "a program of extermination, kidnapping and forced abortion."[10] Only the most perverse form of "logical gerrymandering" allows one to find any relationship between *RuSHA* and *Roe v. Wade.* As reprehensible as *Roe* is and as offensive as abortion on demand is, it does not begin to approach the evil of a nation forcing women to slaughter their children on the basis of racial presuppositions.

The analogy of the Holocaust and the applications of the Nuremberg principles would fit only if a group in the United States were selected for state-mandated abortions, or if abortions were performed against the will of the women involved. If the state decided to solve illegal immigration by requiring all illegal immigrants who were pregnant to have abortions, then *RuSHA* would apply to any doctor or government official participating in such a program. If the state determined that a particular religious group was so objectionable that they must be exterminated, then the *RuSHA* case would apply to anyone participating in the implementation of that plan. There is no such circumstance in the United States today.

The *RuSHA* indictment alleged that the defendants forced Polish women to undergo abortions,[11] which is exactly our argument. It is the forcing of abortion that makes one a criminal under moral law. It is the forcing of abortion that would require Christians to disobey the law. It is the forcing of abortion that would make the principles of Nuremberg apply to the United States. It is the forcing of abortion that would allow the term *holocaust* to be applied legitimately to the United States. Until that takes place, Christians need to find another term to define the evil of abortion on demand in America, and they need to base their rationale for opposing abortion in the Scriptures, not in bad history lessons.

Holocaust Prevented by Law

Hitler came to power on the same premise on which pro-violence anti-abortionists operate: there is a problem and they alone know how to deal with that problem. Pro-violence anti-abortionists require the suspension of the constitutional protection of the accused for their method to succeed, and they are quite willing to suspend that process by force if necessary. The fact that pro-violence anti-abortion activity creates its own "holocaust" (the murder of abortionists) may be more acceptable to its advocates in that it is one of their own creation and of their own choice.[12] Another holocaust will only be prevented by the affirmation of the laws of our land, which are the only defense against genocide and criminality.

To employ lawlessness to uphold the law, even lawlessness toward man's law under the guise of upholding God's law, ultimately destroys all law. It is emotionally satisfying and motivating to decry abortion in America as another holocaust, but it does little to assist Christians to establish biblical and Christ-honoring responses to this evil.

Michael Bray claims, "The ongoing slaughter of unborn children closely parallels the genocide directed at the Jews in Nazi Germany."[13] One of the first responsibilities facing Christians, who intend to act on conviction rather than passion, is to be certain their words mean what they say. The first and best Bible study tool a Christian should learn to use is a dictionary. If Bray had consulted *Webster's*, he would have discovered that calling abortion in America "genocide" reflects his emotions, rather than the definition of the word.

In 1948, the United Nations formulated the Convention on the Prevention and the Punishment of the Crime of Genocide.[14] Article I extended its provision to both peace and war. Article II defined genocide in accordance with the

Nuremberg Charter as "any of the following acts committed with intent to destroy, in whole or in part, a national, ethnical, racial, or religious group, as such: killing members of the group; causing serious bodily or mental harm to members of the group; deliberately inflicting on the group conditions of life calculated to bring about its physical destruction in whole or in part; imposing measures intended to prevent births within the group; forcibly transferring children of the group to another group." [15]

Michael Hirsh commented on genocide, noting, "Barbarisms cannot occur under the rule of law . . . when any executive, legislator, or judge acts out of accord with the rule of law, he is not making a new law but is acting lawlessly. Making statesmen responsible to the law has been the goal . . . since America's beginning." [16] Hirsh's statements are correct, but his application of them to abortion in America is not. Statesmen are subject to the law. Nuremberg and the Genocide Convention both establish that positive law is no excuse for travesties against humanity. Yet, as horrible as abortion is, it is not being used as a tool of genocide in the United States and does not qualify as "genocide" by any legitimate definition. There is no government policy to exterminate a particular group, a necessary component to prove genocide. Abortion is sin, but abortion in America is neither a holocaust nor genocide. The emotionalizing of the issues prevents those affected from examining the question on the basis of the Word of God.

SOCIETY AND SUCCESS OR FAITHFULNESS V. EFFECTIVENESS

PRO-VIOLENCE ANTI-ABORTIONISTS believe Christians are responsible for redeeming society as well as for evangelizing individuals, which places them under great pressure to bring the kingdom of God to pass upon the earth. This causes them to make abortion *the* issue in contemporary society and to make "success" in the "fight" against abortion all important. This is the justification which pro-violence anti-abortionists use for forcing others to accept their beliefs.

The idea that Christians should force others to live by the Word of God has been rejected by Christian leaders. The great reformer, Martin Luther, refused to coerce others to accept his faith. He wrote, "I do not wish to force anyone to believe as I do." He rejected the proposition that it was his responsibility to impose the rule of God upon earth by force. Luther believed that the Second Coming of Jesus Christ would be preceded by the rejection of the rule of both the law of God and the law of man. He did not foresee Christians' imposing the rule of law upon others by force.

Defective Doctrine Leads to Use of Force

Because they believe they are responsible for bringing the kingdom of God to earth, pro-violence anti-abortionists want to impose their views upon others by force rather than attempt to influence them by preaching, praying, and protesting. Some are prepared to impose a theocracy upon America. One advocate of violence threatened, "The state . . . must prohibit non-Christian public worship if it is to maintain a just [that is, Christian] society."[1]

Those who reject the idea of theocracy are accused of compromise. "The smug reply to the exponent of theocracy is usually riddled with the same epithets: Crusades! Inquisition! Salem Witch Trials! . . . superstition and darkness?"[2] Their belief in theocracy justifies their willingness to sacrifice the rights and the lives of individuals with whom they disagree. Michael Bray asks, "Is Biblical law and the burning of witches and Satanists so bad?"[3] Our answer is "Yes!" In a democratic republic, the rights of everyone must be protected for the rights of anyone to be preserved.

The salvation of society is not the goal of Scripture. Jesus respected human government, but He did not express any confidence in it or any responsibility for it as a vehicle for the bringing of the kingdom of God to earth. If government could accomplish anything of ultimate worth, surely it should be able to eliminate poverty. Yet, Jesus said that poverty would be a blight upon mankind until His return (Matt. 26:11). That truth does not make us despair of relief services for the poor, but it does humble us to know that our government will ultimately be ineffective.

Pro-violence anti-abortionists are often driven by a particular view of end-times theology which argues that things are going to get better and better until Christ returns to an earth at peace. End-times theology is a dangerous and unacceptable basis upon which to base public policy. God has not given man the responsibility to establish His kingdom, either in the heart of the individual or upon the earth in general. Man's ability to misunderstand biblical teachings requires that men hold those truths dear, but gently, lest error be imposed upon society.

Abortion as the Issue in America

Consistent with their end-times doctrine and their emotionalization of abortion, pro-violence anti-abortionists have elevated abortion to the status of being *the* issue now facing the church. In his foreword to Randall Terry's *Operation Rescue,* D. James Kennedy called abortion "the issue in this country." Bray also elevated the rescuing of the unborn to the position of being his ultimate concern. He claimed, "We must clutch *THE* issue of the hour [abortion], enduring the heavy costs which ensue." [4]

Violent anti-abortionists have even exalted the saving of the unborn above the concern for the salvation of the souls of others. Bray suggested, "The right to life takes precedence over the . . . code of nonviolence and . . . the evangelization of the abortionist must defer to effective means of rescuing the child." [5] He sets aside the redemptive imperative of the gospel in order to pursue his cultural imperative.

With opposition to abortion exalted to the position of ultimate concern, pro-violence anti-abortionists can subordinate all other ethical considerations to opposing abortion. Elevating the unborn to the position of ultimate concern causes pro-violence anti-abortionists to ignore the rest of Scripture. The Bible, however, states that Christians' ultimate concern must be "to fear God and to keep his commandments" (Eccles. 12:9–13), which places Christians under the whole weight of the biblical revelation including:

- "Love thy neighbour as thyself" (Matt. 22:39)

- "Love your enemies, bless them that curse you, do good to them that hate you, and pray for them which despitefully use you, and persecute you" (Matt. 5:44)

- "Be not overcome of evil, but overcome evil with good" (Rom. 12:21)

- "The wrath of man worketh not the righteousness of God" (James 1:20)

If we make abortion *the* issue in America, we have distorted the biblical mandate for faithfulness. When we make abortion our primary issue and winning becomes our goal, we substitute fruitfulness for the biblical mandate for faithfulness.

Faithfulness and Effectiveness

In his second book, *A Time to Kill,* Bray argues that there is a familiar plague that reads, 'God has not called me to be successful, He has called me to be faithful.' . . . There is . . . a difference between being 'faithful' and being obedient." [6] Bray does not explain either faithfulness or obedience, nor does he explain how one can be faithful and disobedient, or how one can be obedient and unfaithful. Both would be required to make his case. His distinction is contrived and unreal.

If you are faithful, you will be obedient. If you are obedient, you will be faithful (Matt. 25:21, John 14:21, 1 Pet. 1:1–2, Heb. 5:8–9, and 2 Tim. 4:7). Being biblically pro-life—being obedient and faithful—does not necessarily result in stopping abortion—being fruitful or effective. It does result in:

- Reassigning resources for the support of unwed mothers.

- Compassion rather than condemnation for women who are pregnant out of wedlock.

- Rejection of all anti-children attitudes.

- Compassion for women who have had or who are seeking an abortion. [7]

- Brokenheartedness for those who are participating in the abortion industry.

Expulsion or Abortion

A student who was pregnant was dismissed from a Baptist college. At first, it seems that the school is holding up a high standard of sexual morality. However, on closer examination, it becomes obvious that this desire must be balanced by the compassion which will not compromise the truth, but which also will not push someone into an evil practice. Not so subtly, the school tacitly said to other students, "If you quietly get an abortion, you can stay in school, but if you remain pregnant and unwed you will be expelled." Truth and mercy must be balanced; compassion and conviction must be harmonized, if believers are going to maintain a consistent and compelling pro-life stance.

Terrorism and the Fear of God

With abortion being made the sole issue and with winning being made the only goal in the anti-abortion movement, terrorism becomes a synonym for the fear of God. Anxiety over the threat of assault is not the root of the fear of the Lord, nor is it a positive motivation in the lives of men. Nowhere does the Bible encourage Christians to establish biblical principles in society by intimidation.

The fear of God should be a positive influence in the lives of men; fear of violence is a negative influence. The former is redemptive; the latter is retributive. The fear of God is the only motive that will cause men to cease from private and secret sin. The only way in which the fear of God will become a dynamic in the lives of men again is to restore confidence in God as the Creator. Like the sins of Israel, the sins of America stem from a defective view of God.

We all know the bankruptcy of a system where the end is paramount, where any means necessary are acceptable. Throughout the writings of pro-violence anti-abortionists, the term *effectiveness* appears. It was his anxiety over ineffectiveness that drove Randall Terry to abandon the prophetic protest of abortion and to adopt the tactics of Operation Rescue.

Effectiveness is not a basis for accepting a plan that works, and it is not a basis for rejecting a plan that may fail. Pragmatism argues that if it works, it is right—if it fails, it is wrong. Pragmatism has infected the church until she has adopted many of the world's ways, which contradict the gospel she preaches. The world sees, smiles, and rejects the message.

The means-and-ends tension in Christian methodology addresses the fact that Christians are constrained by eternal values and by truth that is eternal. That constraint means that sometimes in this life, in the short run, Christians will lose, knowing that at the Judgment, in the long run, they will win. The means-and-ends tension really addresses motive; it also addresses the difference between being right and being righteous. It is right to oppose abortion; to be righteous one must oppose it with methods and means that are consistent with the character of Christ and the commandments of Scripture.

The End Excuses the Means

Was Michael Griffin justified in killing David Gunn? Hill claimed, "The question of whether Dr. Gunn's death was just could easily be decided by you if your life had been one of those spared by the man who killed Dr. Gunn." Like Bray's approval of the burning of a few witches, Hill's statement is rooted in the ethical fallacy of a good end justifying any means.

Bray asks, "What if the first ten abortuaries . . . had been set ablaze? . . . Would a healthy sense of fear have engendered deterrence if not also a spirit of repentance?"8 Bray confuses repentance with intimidation. The fear of man may cause some to be less public with their evil, because of intimidation, but it will not stop evil.

As an ethical concept, even if it were possible to stop abortion with violence, it would be wrong to do so. What if the physician attending Hitler's mother at the delivery of her child had had a vision showing him the evil Hitler would bring upon the world. Would that physician have been right in putting the infant Hitler to death? Ethically and morally, he would not.

The ethical fallacy in Bray's and Hill's position should be obvious to anyone. The righteousness of an act should be decided upon the merits of the case, both the end and the means, not upon personalities. Self-interest is not the high moral and ethic ground upon which we want to make the kind of decisions that Hill poses for his audience.

In his first novel, John Grisham presented a similar ethical dilemma. Entitled the same as Bray's second book, *A Time to Kill,* Grisham's book related the story of a fictional black father in rural Mississippi who murders two white men who raped his adolescent daughter. When the trial is concluded with the finding that the father was not guilty, one of the jurors explained the decision. When the jury seemed hopelessly deadlocked, a woman on the jury said, "Close your eyes and imagine that the little girl who was raped was white, and that her assailants were black. Imagine that the white father then murdered the two black assailants who raped his white daughter. How would you vote under these circumstances?"

The jury decided unanimously for acquittal. This means of achieving acquittal raises important ethical questions. Is it right to appeal to racism in order to win acquittal of a guilty man whose potential conviction might partially be motivated by racism? Should it make any difference in the eyes of the law if the child were red, yellow, black, or white? Is this not the same racist motive that resulted in the murder of many blacks by the Ku Klux Klan? Does sympathy with the victim dictate our sense of law? Can an outraged father murder men who are guilty?

If winning is everything, then the method doesn't matter. If Christians must win in order to honor God, they will resort to methods that will dishonor Him. But in ethical, moral, and spiritual matters, the end is not everything. No matter how sympathetic we are with the father of a brutalized child, we cannot, we must not excuse the law being taken into the hands of an enraged individual. The same is true of Michael Griffin in his murder of David Gunn and in Paul Hill's murder of Barnett.

In Grisham's novel, the two white men were obviously guilty of a crime against a black child. If they had been interrupted during the assault and been inadvertently killed as the rescuer of the child stopped the assault, the killer would have been innocent of murder. Instead, the assault was after they were taken into custody, therefore their death at the hands of the father was murder.

No matter how opposed the pro-life movement was to what Gunn was doing, it cannot approve of what Griffin did. No matter how opposed the pro-life movement is to abortion, it cannot embrace the criminal madness of Paul Hill. To do so would be a travesty of justice, a breach of the doctrine of the sanctity of human life, and a blow to the credibility of the high moral, spiritual, and ethical grounds that form the basis on which abortion on demand must be opposed.

The limitations upon legitimate acts by believers is the gospel of Christ. The entire world bears the bloodguilt of the Lord Jesus Christ, but the Father of Glory withholds His wrath in a redemptive love for those who will come to Christ. Can we do any less?

Are Christians Required to Succeed?

The logical conclusion of the doctrine of the pro-violence anti-abortionists is that Christians are not called to be faithful; they are required to be fruitful. Yet, the prophets contended that members of the covenant community were bound by a requirement to live justly and to exercise mercy. There was no compulsion for them to force others to exercise justice and mercy.

Jesus demonstrated His confidence in the providence and sovereignty of the Father by not attempting to rectify every wrong on the earth during His incarnation (1 Pet. 2:21–23). This was not due to a callousness toward the sufferings of others, nor to any incapacity on His part. It was due to God's eternal plan. The apostle Paul taught that the kingdom of God's purpose in time was not to rectify all injustice. In 1 Timothy 6, he taught the implications of the gospel in regard to slaves and their owners. He proposed no social activism. In the Book of Philemon, without any threat against his person, Paul appealed to Philemon. He did not say, "If you harm Onesimus, I will kill you." There is no example of "defensive action" in the Gospels, Acts, or the epistles.

For Christians to say, babies are dying every day, and I must stop it at any cost and by any means, is to impugn the compassion and capacity of God. God sees the same thing. God brings His prophets to proclaim the evil of abortion. Yet, God withholds His judgment for His own sovereign purposes—His judgment brings justice at a future time of His choosing. For man to arrogate to himself that which God has reserved for Himself, for man to impose his timetable upon God's eternal design, are acts of pride and humanism, not humility and principle.

11

ADVOCATES OF VIOLENCE

I AM A MEDIA STAR," Paul Hill boasted to a friend in France in the fall of 1993.[1] On July 30, 1994, Americans learned that Hill, who claimed to be a Presbyterian minister, had murdered Dr. John Britton in Pensacola, Florida. As police led him away from the murder scene, Hill reportedly said, "I know one thing: No innocent babies are going to be killed in that clinic today." He now sits on death row in a Florida prison awaiting execution.

Hill had been arrested in June 1993 for violating noise ordinances when he stood outside an abortion clinic shouting, "Mommy, please don't let them kill me." Born in Miami on February 6, 1954, he graduated from Belhaven College in Jackson, Mississippi, in 1977, and in 1983 he received a master of divinity from the Reformed Theological Seminary in Jackson. Hill was ordained by the Presbyterian Church of America at the Palmetto Presbytery in Kingstree, South Carolina. In 1989, Hill changed denominations and became pastor of a congregation in Lake Worth, Florida, that was affiliated with the Orthodoxy Presbyterian Church. In 1990, he was "divested without censure" from this church because of doctrinal disagreements.

Hill moved to Pensacola and joined Trinity Presbyterian Church of Valparaiso, Florida. He talked increasingly about violence against abortionists and founded Defensive Action.

He carried signs that said Execute Abortionists and publicly supported Michael Griffin's murder of Dr. David Gunn.

In June 1993, Trinity Presbyterian excommunicated Hill, but indicated he could be readmitted if he changed his views on violence against abortion providers. It was then, working as an auto detailer, that Hill seemed to become preoccupied with doing something significant to stop abortion in Pensacola. A longtime friend recalled, "To me this is the crux of the story; he's there waxing cars, and he believes he's been called to do something more with his life."

Although his actions shocked millions, Hill himself had already justified his actions in his preaching and publications. He had appealed to his own Presbyterian tradition to justify his actions, even though the Presbyterian Church of America had refuted his claims and excluded him from the ministry. Before committing the murder, Hill defended his actions in an unpublished manuscript entitled "Defensive Action," the first section of which asked two fundamental questions:

- What responsibility does the individual have toward his neighbor if his neighbor's life is about to be taken by force?

- May we use force to protect unborn children from imminent death even if the government forbids us to do so? [2]

Hill answered the first question by saying, "You must take all action necessary to protect innocent life." He answered the second by quoting Acts 5:29: "The child of God 'must obey God rather than men.'"

Hill and the Presbyterian Church of America

Hill defended his beliefs and actions by appealing to the Westminster Catechism, which was written in 1647 and has exercised enduring influence among Presbyterians. In discussing his second fundamental question, Hill quoted from a position paper by the Presbyterian Church of America (PCA), which declared, "Nevertheless, when the state, or any other authority, commands one to do what is contrary to what the Law of God requires, or to refrain from doing what the Law of God commands, the Christian 'must obey God rather than men' (Acts 5:29b)." [3]

The key condition is, "when the state commands one to do what is contrary to what the law of God requires." The PCA is correct. When secular authorities compel evil, such as requiring women to have abortions, then it is time to oppose the law. When the secular authority forbids the practice of one's faith, for example, ruling that the Bible cannot be read in one's home, it is time to oppose the law decisively, but not violently.

Neither of these cases apply in the United States. No one is required to have an abortion. No woman is restricted from practicing her faith in bringing to term any baby, no matter how deformed or unwanted. Yet, Hill repeatedly misapplied the PCA statement and continually referred to it to support his position.

In addition, the Old Testament law of retaliation has been superseded by the law of reconciliation, which is summarized by Jesus as loving God and loving one's neighbor. For Hill, the reality with which he must live is that Gunn and Britton were as much his neighbors as the innocent babies he wished to save. It is impossible to accept one's relationship with one human with whom you have no connection (unborn babies) and to reject your relationship with another whom you don't know (abortion providers).

In a democratic republic, when a majority of the people oppose a law, that law will be changed. The only laws that can be enforced in a secular society are those laws that the majority are willing to obey voluntarily. Yet this does not permit anyone to interfere with another who voluntarily and willfully practices what is allowed by a provision of law, no matter how evil one might believe that practice to be.

When law is ignored by anyone impudently—even when motivated by religious passion—the occasion awaits for someone with a "violent zeal" for a law of their own imagination, which I may violate, to take the law into his own hands and judge me guilty with a bullet. The tragedy is that the pro-violent anti-abortionist's logic, followed to its reasonable conclusion, could result in pro-life activists finding themselves shot down by pro-abortion activists. Where would this stop?

Requiring Christians to employ physical violence in opposing abortion certainly violates the spirit of the Word of God and of the Lord Jesus Christ. It also places the Christian in the position of violating the Fifth Commandment— thou shalt not kill—in a misguided effort to coerce others to obey the commandment. Furthermore, Christians cannot take the law of God into their own hands to oppose evil, they cannot go further than God allows.

Who Are God's Judges?

God used Jehu to bring judgment upon Ahab and Jezebel (2 Kings 10:1–14). Jehu went further than God commanded, consequently, rather than being remembered as the instrument of God's judgment, he awaits judgment for his sin (Hos. 1:2–4).

The Babylonians were used of God to judge Israel. The Babylonians believed they could do anything they wanted because of the sins of Israel. They said, "We offend not, because they have sinned against the Lord, the habitation of justice, even the Lord, the hope of their fathers" (Jer. 50:7). The pride of Babylonia, the instrument of His judgment, was a greater offense to God than the sin of Israel (Jer. 50:18, 20, 31–46).

Man cannot exercise judgment as he will. He can only do what God commands and cannot without personal penalty go further than God commanded. Both Jehu and the Babylonians learned this to their harm. Pro-violence anti-abortionists will discover the same truth when they stand before a holy God.

Hill's Concept of Role Distinction

Hill's ignorance of the gospel is nowhere more obvious than when he voices a version of Bray's concept of "role distinction." He claimed, "Christ had a direct command from God that He should offer His life as an atoning sacrifice. His case was unique. We have no such command. We have the God-given responsibility to take defensive action to protect life." All Scripture contradicts these notions.

Jesus Christ is God. He was born of a virgin, has an impeccable character, lived a sinless life, died an atoning death, and was resurrected on the third day. Yet Christ's life was a pattern for believers. Revelation 12:11 declares the victory of the believer in this world, and nowhere is it said that they overcame the enemy by militancy or violence. First Peter 2:21–23 states that Jesus left us an example of suffering. No one was more innocent than He. The angels had been charged with His protection and defense since His conception (Ps. 91:11–12). Yet, beginning at Caiaphas's court, He was allowed to be assaulted physically without defense. A higher principle than self-defense was active. It is my belief that the angels begged God to let them deliver Jesus.4 They could not imagine that any good could come from His death. Yet, had He not died, we could not live. If He had been rescued, we would have perished.

While God has not orchestrated the abortion mill in America, He was not taken by surprise by it either. It is *His* sovereign responsibility to bring good out of it (Rom. 8:28). It is my responsibility to obey His life and His Word. The killing of abortion providers does not do that. As much as I might want to rescue those babies by any means, like the angels, we are restrained by the word of the Father. He knows what He is doing, and in His time we, like the angels, will understand. We must protest the evil of abortion. We must publicize the evil of abortion, but we must not break God's law by disobeying the noncoercive laws of men.

The Ku Klux Klan

Repeatedly, pro-violence anti-abortionists refer to the Civil War as an example of "defensive action." The post-Civil War era produced the best illustration of a "defensive action" committee, as envisioned by Paul Hill. Through the Ku Klux Klan, southern Christians, under the guise of preserving "Christian culture," persecuted, murdered, and terrorized those with whom they disagreed. Christ gave no "command" that Christians form such committees. In fact, it is obvious that these committees are contrary to His teachings.

In addition, individual vigilante actions, which we would call terrorism and Hill would call "defensive action," are also excluded by the doctrine of Christ. Unfortunately for the entire pro-life movement, the legitimate protest against abortion, the legitimate publicizing of the evil of abortion, and the legitimate pressing for the change of abortion laws through the political process are now discredited because of the actions of Griffin and Hill.

Christians must not allow their legitimate indignation at the evil of abortion to cause them to accept unbiblical methods and means of opposing that evil. If the teachings of Christ mean anything, it is that men are constrained by eternal values and by eternal truth. That constraint means that sometimes in this life, in the short run, they will lose, knowing that at the judgment, in the long run, they will win.

The Cornerstone of Democracy

The cornerstone of our democratic republic is that a person is innocent until proved guilty. While that principle may seem aggravating at times, particularly when the guilt of another seems so obvious, no thoughtful person would seriously wish to sacrifice this remarkably biblical concept. Numbers 35 establishes the weight of evidence required to declare a person guilty and enable society to execute them. There is no provision in the Scripture for unilateral, individual vigilante action to take another person's life.

In a society run by and ruled by sinners, errors will occur. In a society where the sanctity of human life is the ruling principle, the excess of a guilty person occassionally escaping punishment is the price of assuring that an innocent person is not punished. The balance obviously is, if too often the guilty go free, contempt for the law results. If, however, the innocent are found guilty routinely, despair results. Both are lethal to a biblically-based criminal justice system, even one administered by sinners.

Hill was so preoccupied with punishing the guilty that he proposed a system that would remove all safeguards for the innocent. His "defensive action," shortsighted as it was, would appear to protect one group of innocents and expose another group to harm. It is not legitimate for Christians to ignore the needs of the innocent unborn, but in pursuing their protection and deliverance, they must not compromise the innocents who are already born. They must not bring the innocent baby into a society jaded by the denial of human rights, produced by the pro-life movement's denial of civil rights to those with whom they disagree.

While Hill may imagine that his system reestablishes God's design for justice, it, in fact, does just the opposite. Rather than restore this country to a biblically-based system of justice, Hill's proposals would remove the only vestige of Christian principle that remains in our legal system, namely, the careful controls for the protection of the innocent. As is so often the case, well-motivated Christians, unconstrained by the Word of God, invite disaster upon themselves, the cause of Christ, and upon their country.

The arrogance of Hill's proposal is his willingness to assume that he alone or his friends and he alone can determine guilt that is worthy of death. If Hill could ever agree that there were a single instance where he or his friends could make a mistake and assume someone was guilty who was actually innocent, then his entire system would fail.

Any system based on the absolute necessity for the punishment of all the guilty is a system that rushes toward totalitarianism. The only system that can guarantee the punishment of all the guilty is a system where one, and only one, assesses guilt and innocence, and he does it with absolute and unappealable authority. Among humans such a system is totalitarianism. The logical extension of Hill's proposal is a totalitarianism of terrorism.

Michael Bray on Force in the Pro-life Movement

"Could you kill an abortionist, Reverend Bray?" "I have no plans to," he answered.[5] "Could you pull the trigger, Reverend Bray?" asked the *Baltimore Sun* on October 9, 1994. Bray responded, "I could . . . as to whether I would—I may."[6] In a subsequent *Houston Post* story, Bray was quoted as saying that he had "'no plans' to oppose abortion violently."[7] Paul Hill made similar statements a year before he murdered Britton and his escort.

Bray and Hill both supported Michael Griffin after his shooting of David Gunn, and Bray visited with Hill after his shooting of an abortionist and his escort. Bray argued that "the godly use of force is easily demonstrated from Scripture."[8] In *A Time to Kill,* he wrote, "There are many examples of a use of force to accomplish a purpose in the Old Testament." [9] To support his argument, Bray examined the life of Moses.

Moses and the Egyptian

"Moses is given high marks as a man of faith," Bray noted. He then argues that Moses' killing of an Egyptian was just, because the Scripture never condemns it.[10] The real evidence of Moses' righteousness, however, is found in Hebrews 11:26, which states, "esteeming the reproach of Christ greater riches than the treasures in Egypt." This was an act of faith. Moses' righteousness was due to his faith, not an act of force or violence. To find support for violence against transgressors of the law in Hebrews 11, Bray must deal with those who "not accepting deliverance; that they might obtain a better resurrection" (Heb. 11:35). He must also deal with those described in Hebrews 11:36–40. Most of those commended by God in Hebrews 11 were exalted because of their suffering for Christ, not because they tried to force anyone to obey Him.

Moses' endorsement by God, like David's, Josiah's and Peter's, did not have to do with God's ignoring or justifying their errors. It had to do with their heart. These flawed men were loved by God. The example that we should draw from their lives is not of violence against those who oppose the gospel, but of God's love for fallen men.

It is this writer's judgment that Moses' action was wrong, as his attempt to hide the body of the Egyptian and his initial rejection as a leader by his own people both indicated. It took forty years of wilderness exile before Moses was ready for leadership. In most states today, a manslaughter conviction results in a sentence less than five years. Moses' exile for forty years seems harsh in comparison. To God, it was just. Yet, those forty years of exile hardly justify the conclusion that God approved of Moses' action.

Sword of the Spirit

The Word of God says, "Choose you this day whom ye will serve" (Josh. 24:15). All the prophets affirm this statement. God did not send Jonah to Ninevah with an automatic weapon to coerce compliance with His will. God did not send Jonah with a sword. God sent him with the "sword of the Spirit, which is the Word of God" (Eph. 6:17). The people had a choice.

Without a clear hermeneutic that distinguishes between the reality of Old Testament history and its application in the lives of believers today, pro-violence anti-abortionists fall into a quagmire of confusion and contradiction. The Old Testament is true, but its purpose was to prepare the New Covenant (1 Cor. 10:6ff; Rom. 15:4). Nothing has been set aside, but now believers can understand the truth behind Old Testament events. The purpose of Old Testament events was never the forcing of anyone to live by God's law.

Jonah preached judgment and justice, but he never imagined it was his responsibility to bring such to pass. Initially, the opportunity for repentance that God gave to the people of Ninevah depressed Jonah. He wanted the people of Ninevah to be judged. God had to teach Jonah of His mercy. Like Bray, Jonah misunderstood the God of the Old Testament, who was a God of mercy and forgiveness. God chose not to make man a puppet. Men, even well-motivated men who love God's ways, cannot choose to do that which God has not chosen to do, for example, force men to love Him, which means forcing them to obey him.

Was Jesus Violent?

Bray accuses Jesus of violent action, observing, "He had occasion to act forcefully (see John 2:13–22; Mark 11:15–21)."[11] Jesus' indignation in cleansing the temple is instructive for Christians. Its application, however, would not be for abortionists, but rather toward the Laodicean church and its indifference and complacency. Furthermore, Jesus did not physically harm anyone in cleansing the temple. Bray's application of this passage of Scripture is not supported by any other teacher of the gospel.

Bray's interpretation of Luke 22:33–35 elevates the physical above the spiritual, which leads him to argue, "The burden of proof is upon those who would deny that force can be applied morally."[12] No one would deny that force can be morally used by a Christian. What is denied is that force should be used to impose our faith upon another. What is denied is that force should be used in a democratic republic to impose religious convictions against abortion upon a secular society. Christians can change the laws of the land. They can preach and prophesy, but Christians cannot and should not terrorize, intimidate, or coerce others to obey the truth. God does not do that, and Christians cannot and should not do that.

Paul's greatest desire was that those whom he discipled would continue to obey when he had left them (Phil. 2:12). His desire was that others would obey because of love, not coercion. There is no love in a coerced response either on the part of the one who obeys or the one who is obeyed. Love demands and requires voluntary obedience.

Christians are to live as Christ lived—loving the helpless, the heathen, and those who hate us.[13] This way of living does not mean that we are pacifists. It does mean that we love those who cannot help themselves, those who are breaking God's laws, and those who are warring against

God. We love them by telling them the truth—God will forgive them. We love them by trying to meet needs in their lives. We love them by telling them that God will condemn them if they persist in rebellion, and we leave that condemnation to God.

Bray quoted Reinhold Niebuhr, who pointed out a theological flaw of modern pacifism.[14] He would have done better to point out Niebuhr's famous statement about democracy: "Man's capacity for justice makes democracy possible; but man's inclination to injustice makes democracy necessary."[15] It is the "inclination to injustice" of well-intentioned, misguided souls, such as Bray, that makes it impossible and unwise to trust their vision for America. That which is worth defending with force is the right of every man to pursue his own faith and the right of every man to preach, publicize, and promote his faith.

What is unworthy of the use of force is any effort to impose one's faith upon another, and this would include an expression and/or application of that faith. Without doubt, the one time when force is excluded absolutely from the life of the believer is in the advancement of the kingdom of God. If the Crusades, the Inquisition, and the Salem witch trials taught us anything, it is that conversion by fire does nothing for the eternal destiny of men and women.

God Calls Men and Women

Bray claimed that those who attack abortion providers have been called by God, suggesting, "We respect . . . the calling that God may well have made upon the lives of Christians like Michael Griffin and Shelly Shannon."[16] It is impossible to "respect" someone's claim to having been called by God unless you believe they have been. You can have confidence that others have been called by God when:

- They act in accordance with the Word of God.

- They act in such a way as to bring honor and glory to God.

- They act in such a way as to bring others to a saving knowledge of Christ.

- They act in such a way as to inspire others to greater devotion to Christ.

- They expose the sin of a people or a nation in such a way that sinners are confronted with their need to repent.

When Jim Elliot and his comrades were killed by the Auca Indians in Ecuador in 1956, each of these things happened. The secular world stood in awe of their sacrifice because they could not understand it. Thousands have been saved and challenged by the examples of these martyrs. No one has been saved and no one has been challenged to deeper devotion to Christ by the actions of Griffin or Hill or by the rhetoric of Bray or Trosch.

"If Doctors Must Die . . ."

In the summer of 1993, Father David Trosch, an Alabama parish priest, attempted to place an ad in a Pensacola newspaper that recommended the killing of abortion doctors. Trosch's archbishop ordered him to stop any public discussion of his ideas. Trosch refused and was relieved from his parish church. There followed an extensive correspondence with the archbishop, the Vatican, and other U.S. bishops in which Trosch accused all of them of compromise for not supporting his position. After Paul Hill's July 1994 assault on John B. Britton, Trosch said that if a hundred doctors must die that was a small price to pay for saving thousands of babies. He also suggested that the killing of abortion doctors would begin a "holocaust" that would bring abortion to an end.

One of the principle deficiencies of the use of Scripture by all of the advocates of violence in the pro-life movement is that they come to Scripture with a dogmatic presupposition. They then look for Scriptures that they believe support their arguments. Several of them have said to this author, "I am trying out this new argument." They have not determined to obey Scripture, rather they have determined to find in Scripture justification for what they have already decided to do. Pro-violence anti-abortionists are not alone in employing this hermeneutical method, but they are consistent in practicing it. Trosch is no exception.

In a July 7, 1994, letter Trosch wrote, "If you have some other immediately effective alternative method, of saving condemned innocent children, I, and others, are more than willing to listen."[17] Here Trosch falls into the same ethical dilemma that has been pointed out before, namely, justifying one's means to achieve a particular goal. When he assigns to himself responsibility for successfully stopping abortion and successfully stopping it now, he ceases to be guided by Scripture and becomes oppressed by his own passion. It is unnecessary to have an answer to the question, How can I stop abortion right now?, to determine a godly and biblical response to this evil. *Pragmatism*—it will work—and *expediency*—it will work now—are not the high ethical, moral, and spiritual grounds on which Christians make their judgments.

In a June 20, 1994, letter to Joseph Cardinal Ratzinger, head of the Vatican's Sacred Congregation for the Doctrine of the Faith, Trosch explained, "The abortionist, who is a practicing murderer, should be stopped from continuing his evil practice. If this means that his life must be terminated, because other deterrents are not immediately effective . . . then it should be terminated with prudent dispatch."[18] Trosch's confusion of canon, biblical, criminal, and civil law creates an almost impossible moral and ethical morass. According to canon and biblical law, abortionists are murderers. According to civil and criminal law in the United States, they are not. According to canon and biblical law, the practices of abortionists are evil. According to civil and criminal law, they are not. According to canon and biblical law, the practices of abortionists will be judged by God, and He will punish them for their evil practice. According to civil and criminal law, no penalty will be assessed against abortionists. If Christians are to have a righteous response to abortion-on-demand, they must keep these distinctions in mind.

In a July 25, 1994, letter, Trosch suggested, "One of the most evil beliefs is that a murderer of innocent children should not have his or her life terminated when extinction of his life would save, at least for the time being, the lives of innocent persons."[19] A private citizen cannot legally nor legitimately pass a death sentence upon anyone. Such an idea is contrary to all law, both the law of man and the law of God. Even in the theocratic case law of the Old Testament, the community of faith had to agree with the sentence of death. No individual had that right, even in a theocracy.

Trosch's Use of Scripture

Trosch principally builds his case for violence on the Transfiguration (Matt. 17:1–9; Mark 9:1–10; Luke 9:27–36) in which three were seen in a transfigured form: the lawgiver—Moses, the prophet—Elijah, and Jesus Christ—the fulfillment of the law and the prophets. Three disciples witnessed the Transfiguration: Peter, James, and John.

Trosch argues that the Transfiguration embraces two Old Testament practitioners of violence as role models for Christians. Moses killed an Egyptian, and Elijah slew four hundred prophets of Baal. Furthermore, he argues, Peter's presence at the Transfiguration endorses violence because Trosch contends that Peter killed Ananias and Saphira. Is it not possible, he asks, to deduce that God is endorsing the lives of those who have killed or murdered in a just cause?

This bizarre interpretation of the Transfiguration contradicts the spirit of Jesus, who taught that love for God and love for men fulfills the law and the prophets (Matt. 7:12, 8:21–35, 22:36–40; Rom. 13:8–10; Luke 10:25–37). Through-out His earthly life, Jesus held up love and forgiveness as the fulfillment of the laws of retaliation and vengeance. Trosch's interpretation of the Transfiguration raises some questions that we must answer.

How Well Did Peter Understand the Transfiguration?

Each Gospel account of the transfiguration gives a different insight into Peter's character. Matthew demonstrated that Peter did not yet understand the implications of the presence of Moses, Elijah, and Christ, and records: "Then answered Peter, and said unto Jesus, Lord, it is good for us to be here: if thou wilt, let us make here three tabernacles; one for thee, and one for Moses, and one for Elijah" (Matt. 17:4). Peter did not understand that honor belonged only to the Lord Jesus Christ as the consummation of the law and the prophets. The law and the prophets were not being set aside by Christ; they were being fulfilled in Him.

Luke gives the fullest explanation of Peter's participation in the transfiguration of Christ (Luke 9:32–34). He shows Peter's humanity, because he is asleep at a critical time. Peter was always subject to spiritual lassitude, or slothfulness, as noted in Jesus' arrest in Gethsemane (Matt. 26:37–45).

Luke showed Peter's humanity by showing that his understanding was faulty. Peter did not know what he was saying when he proposed three tabernacles. How often does a subordinate, not understanding the vision and mission of his leader, attempt to ingratiate himself to the leader by excessive zeal, thereby exposing his ignorance of the leader's purpose? Luke showed Peter's humanity by indicating that God ignored Peter. Luke reported, "While he thus spake . . . " (Luke 9:34). God did not even answer Peter, and it was obvious Peter did not yet understand the nature of Christ's mission.

Peter's humanity was manifested at the same time Christ's deity was being declared. To ignore that Jesus Christ is the central character of the Transfiguration is to repeat Peter's error. The homage paid by Moses and Elijah to Christ and all three's ignoring of Peter, James, and John discredits Trosch's suggestion. Any attempt to derive anything about killing of men from the Transfiguration account, displaces Christ from center stage in the episode.

What Is the Meaning of the Transfiguration?

The transfiguration was meant to demonstrate:

- the summation of the law and the prophets in Christ.

- the supremacy of Christ to the law and the prophets.

- the submission of the law and the prophets to Christ.

To ignore that Christ's repeated synthesis of the law and the prophets in the "new commandment of love" is to ignore the entire gospel. The Transfiguration declared as clearly as any event that the significance of the law and the prophets would now have to be examined in the light of the life of Christ. The only implication of Moses and Elijah being present is their representation of the law and the prophets, not their personal conduct. Also, Peter's role in the church, as great as it was, must be balanced by the reality of Galatians 2:11–14.

Did Peter Kill Ananias and Sapphira?

The Bible never suggests that Peter killed Ananias and Sapphira. Peter pronounced God's judgment; he did not execute that judgment. The wording of Acts 5:5 is clear. Peter did not curse Ananias nor did he damn him. Peter judged Ananias's actions, saying, "thou hast not lied unto men, but unto God" (Acts 5:4b). Peter did not desire Ananias's death; he did not recommend his death; he did not even know that God was going to kill Ananias. When Peter told Sapphira of God's judgment, he only reported to her what had happened (Acts 5:9). Peter did not curse Sapphira, and he did not kill her. He only announced God's judgment and awaited God's exercise of that judgment. To make Peter the proximal cause of the death of Ananias and Sapphira is to commit the grossest form of eisogesis.

Should We Slay False Prophets?

Elijah's association with the slaying of the Baal prophets (1 Kings 18:40) has no relevance to contemporary society as an encouragement to violence. The theocratic society in which Elijah functioned has no modern corollary, not even in modern Israel. The attempt to draw anything but spiritual lessons and implications from this experience will cause Christians to miss the point and violate the law of Christ. Even if the exact circumstances applied today— four hundred Satan worshipers make a blood sacrifice in a public ceremony—Christians could not justify their murder. Where they break the law, they can be charged. Believers, however, cannot break the law to oppose evil when that evil is not compelled by the law.

The weakness of Trosch's argument is seen by his statement, "The larger argument to support the use of defensive action to protect the innocent is the silence of Scripture."[20] There are few hermeneutical principles more bankrupt than the argument from silence. To assume a right to take the life of another without judicial or executive responsibility in a democratic republic because Scripture does not specifically deny that right is the height of eisogesis and arrogance. It is the foundation of anarchy. Hill, Bray, and Trosch, the principle spokesmen for violence against abortion providers, distort the Word of God and the life of the Lord Jesus Christ to support their position.

12

WHO CAN USE FORCE?

IS THERE A TIME when a Christian should use force to advance the kingdom of God? Is it ever right for a Christian intentionally and individually to kill another human being because he believes that person is doing wrong? These are the critical questions that must be answered to refute the arguments of pro-violence anti-abortionists.

When Jesus was rejected at Samaria, the disciples asked His permission to call fire down from heaven to punish those who refused to honor Him. Jesus replied, "The Son of man is not come to destroy men's lives, but to save them" (Luke 9:56). In the Garden of Gethsemane, when Peter was prepared to defend Jesus with force, Jesus told him, "Put up thy sword into the sheath: the cup which my Father hath given me, shall I not drink it?" (John 18:11). Matthew recorded another aspect of the conversation: "Put up again thy sword into his place: for all they that take the sword shall perish with the sword" (Matt. 26:52).

These were not time-dated pronouncements by our Lord. They are consistent with all of the Word of God which indicates that we shall reap what we sow, and that angry words engender angry responses. Therefore, Jesus said, "If you use force to solve your problems, then you will provoke others to use force to solve theirs."

When Jesus was on trial before Pilate, He said, "My kingdom is not of this world: if my kingdom were of this world, then would my servants fight, that I should not be delivered to the Jews: but now is my kingdom not from hence. . . . To this end was I born, and for this cause came I into the world, that I should bear witness unto the truth. Every one that is of the truth heareth my voice" (John 18:36–37).

Many pro-violence anti-abortionists would discount the significance of this passage with their doctrine of "role distinction" and their argument that the Greek of this text[1] indicates that Jesus merely addressed the fact that the origin of His kingdom was not of this world. Neither argument is satisfactory. Certainly, the origin of Jesus' kingdom is not this world, but neither are its end or methods. Jesus' kingdom is still not of this world, and His prohibition of violence as a method of that kingdom still applies to His disciples.

The Spirit of Jesus

In the description Jesus gives of Himself in Matthew 11:28–30, He said, "Take my yoke upon you, and learn of me; for I am meek and lowly in heart: and ye shall find rest unto your souls. For my yoke is easy, and my burden is light" (v. 29). In this passage, Jesus describes His relationship to the Father—toward Whom He was "meek," the Son —toward Whom He was "humble," the saved—toward Whom He was "gentle." Jesus was meek toward the Father in that He accepted the will, way, and word of God without question or complaint. He was humble ("lowly") toward Himself in His incarnation. His *kenosis* resulted in no diminution of His divine personage, but He did surrender His divine prerogatives and His divine power, making Him dependent upon the Father. As a result, Jesus confessed, "I can of mine own self do nothing" (John 5:30).[2]

In Jesus, meekness toward God and humility toward self produced gentleness toward others. *Gentleness* means that you care more for the success of others than you do for yourself. This compelled Christ to become poor that His followers might be rich; it enabled Him to become a servant that their needs might be served, and it enabled Him to be patient until they had had the time to be conformed to His nature and character.

Jesus' character has never changed. Although Jesus reigns now as the Lord of lords and as the King of kings, He still delights in the will of the Father, He still desires to exalt the Father above Himself, and He is still gentle toward men. At the Judgment, His fury will be declared, but at present He remains patient and gentle toward men.

The apostle Paul had this same gentleness to others. He compared himself to a nurse who selflessly cared for her charges (1 Thess. 2:7). Paul never suggested that he would take the life of another; he, like his Lord, only proclaimed his willingness to lay down his life for them.

The spirit of Christ is not aggressive, militaristic, nor violent. The heart of Jesus is the heart of One Who loves enough to endure the errors of others until they have the opportunity to repent. It is the heart of One Who trusts the Father enough to know that ultimately all evil will be judged, but judged by the Father and by His word.

This continuing dynamic of the kingdom of God was seen in that Paul's commendations of others never resulted from their aggressiveness or hostility to others, only to their being servants. Based on the character of Christ, Paul admonishes all believers to be "blameless and harmless" (Phil. 2:15). According to the apostle, Christians are to lead others to Christ through the "light" of their faith; they are not to be lighters of fuses.

Christians are to be salt, which does not mean they should employ violence. Paul was willing to be a sacrifice, not a swordsman. When he commended a believer whom he said emulated the character of Jesus Christ, it was Timothy (Phil. 2:19–23) who in his humility and single-mindedness reflected the character of the Lord Jesus Christ. This is the character of the gentle man of God who is not driven by his passions to avenge or to redress every error upon the earth until God's time.

Nowhere do Paul, Peter, John, or Jesus commend force or recommend violence in the kingdom of God. Yet, Jesus did not establish pacifism for all human circumstances. He did establish that violence would have no place in the bringing in of His kingdom upon this earth or in the establishing of His law as the law of the land. The dynamic of the kingdom of God, established by Jesus Christ when He rejected the use of force to usher in His kingdom on earth, is that evil is to be overcome by good, which is the divine nature.

I Beg to Differ with Violent Zeal and Defensive Action

The depth and quality of a man's life cannot be seen by his willingness to force others to accept the truth as he sees it, even if he sees it correctly. The depth and quality of a Christian's life will be seen in how he deals with three groups: those who hate him, those who have harmed him or who wish to harm him, and those who hold views contrary to his own. Jesus Christ came to save those who are without strength (Rom. 5:6), who are sinners (Rom. 5:8), and who are even the very enemies of God (Rom. 5:10).

God's will is that His people will love the same group of people. It is noteworthy that the three groups mentioned above include all men. When Christians love these groups, they actually love themselves. These are those whom Christians are to receive—to take into our hearts and make room for—in the same way that Christ has received

Christians, which brought glory to God (Rom. 15:7). This is the way to God's glory. Here is the way to the kingdom of God on earth, which is in the heart. Christians should leave judgment, retribution, and restoration to God as we live the life of Christ in this day. This is not an admonition to compromise or to moral pacifism. It is an admonition to have the courage to live as Christ lived.

Prophets, Not Vigilantes

Ezekiel describes how God's chosen people had abandoned their devotion to Him (Ezek. 16:1–58). One evidence of their infidelity was that they had sacrificed their own children. Yet, as evil and as wicked as child sacrifice was, God did not begin a vigilante effort to stop it. He called His people to repentance and to return to Him as "the first and vital necessity of their lives" (1 Chron. 28:9).

Later Ezekiel reports that "certain of the elders of Israel came to inquire of the LORD, and sat before me" (Ezek. 20:1). God recited His charges against Israel, charges that included causing the firstborn to "pass through the fire" (vv. 26 and 31). Centuries earlier God had instituted the redemption of the firstborn (Exod. 13:12), an act that distinguished the Israelites from the pagans. Firstborn sons of Israel were to be consecrated to Jehovah as a sacrifice, not by slaying and burning upon altars as dead sacrifices, but as living sacrifices. Inasmuch as the first birth represented all births, the whole nation was to consecrate itself to Jehovah and present itself as a priestly nation in the consecration of the firstborn.

The Israelites disobeyed God. Jeremiah reports, "And they . . . cause[d] their sons and their daughters to pass through the fire unto Molech; which I commanded them not, neither came it into my mind" (Jer. 32:35). Few things manifested the apostasy of Israel as did the sacrifice of their children. The conclusions of Ezekiel 20 and Jeremiah 32, however, promise redemption, not retribution. It is in the context of man's most heinous sins that the glory of God's redemption is declared.

The primary concern of both prophets was the relationship of Israel with her God, not with a particular manifestation of her abandonment of God. For the prophet to substitute anything for the love and worship of God, even an extreme example of apostasy, would itself be idolatrous.

For the pro-violence anti-abortionists or for any Christian to substitute opposition to some manifestation of the apostasy of modern man for his opposition to man's neglect of the love and worship of God is itself idolatrous. Man's chief concern must be his relationship with God. When that relationship is right, the manifestations of the failure of that relationship will disappear.

The prophets declared the evil of the people's rejection of God, but they also preached repentance as the solution. They never focused upon just one of the manifestations of that rejection, and they never suggested that a program of social action focused on one manifestation of evil would end the apostasy. God did not command Ezekiel or Jeremiah to destroy Israel because of infanticide. Rather, He framed His redemption in the context of this sin.

What should be the Christian response to child slaughter, abortion, infanticide, child molestation, child abuse, or child neglect? It should be the preaching of the Cross while protesting the evil of our day. The ultimate solution to abortion in America will be the revival of a personal passion for God among His people, not attacking those who do not know Him and who have no desire to know Him.

God's ultimate judgment of abortionists and their collaborators will be the same today as of the rebels in the Babylonian captivity: "And I will purge out from among you the rebels, and them that transgress against me: I will bring them forth out of the country where they sojourn, and they shall not enter into the land of Israel: and ye shall know that I am the LORD" (Ezek. 20:38). That judgment, however, is neither the right nor the responsibility of Christians.

When Can Christians Use Force?

The following is a reasonable approach to the use of force by Christians.

- Christians may use force to defend themselves, to defend someone for whom they have responsibility, or to defend a stranger whom they see being assaulted. This does not require nor allow them to go looking for those who are being assaulted. Neither does this allow Christians to interfere with another person who is voluntarily choosing to do something the law allows even though it violates the Christian's convictions.

- Christians may use force to defend their country in a just war.

- Christians may use force to restrain someone for whom they have responsibility from self-destructive behavior. Christian parents, for example, might physically restrain their child from using illegal drugs.

Michael Bray, however, extends the use of force to being a "necessary restraint upon evil." [3] He assumes that a nation will not listen to the preaching of the Word of God, and therefore he believes it is necessary to intimidate people from practicing that which is contrary to the Word of God. Bray's conclusions assume a society with no method for redress of grievances.

In an autocratic and/or tyrannical governmental system, this might be true, but this is not true in the United

States. A number of freedoms—the press, speech, religion, lawful assembly—provide avenues for the legal and nonviolent redress of grievances. For the securing of these freedoms and for their inviolable protection, the society simply asks that the citizenry eschew violence. This is a legitimate trade-off and one that Christians should honor. The constraints on violence are the opportunities for redressing grievances, notably, the civil courts, the ballot box, and the street corner.

The challenge for us is not to be blinded by our culture but to allow God's word to speak its eternal truth to a temporal application. In protecting the rights of the most radical element within our society we protect the rights of all. The only demand that is made is that those radical elements employ only nonviolent, legal means in expressing their views.

To Judge, One Must Be Innocent

Pro-violence anti-abortionists claim the right to execute a person who commits abortion. The only grounds for such a claim to judge others is one's own innocence. Even in a secular society, the state accuses the criminal, not the victim's family. This protects the accused from irrational vindictiveness and assumes that only the state is innocent of the crime in question, and is therefore capable of making the accusation.

Officers of the court—judges, attorneys, policemen—are held to high standards of personal conduct because God's design is that the only person who can accuse another is one who is innocent. If the court—the collective representative of all of those involved in the judiciary—or the society are guilty as a group, if they have been corrupted, then respect is lost for the law. They have sacrificed their presumption of innocence and, therefore, their right to judge.

This presumption of innocence on the part of the court is not lost because officers of the court have decided against the opinion of one group or another. It is lost when they capriciously ignore the rule of law and judge by their personal prejudice or for their personal profit.

Jesus taught His disciples that their righteousness must exceed that of the scribes and Pharisees (Matt. 5:20). Yet He warned His disciples that they were no more righteous than the Galileans, whom Pilate had slain, or the eighteen "upon whom the tower in Siloam fell" (Luke 13:1–5). Laying the groundwork for His disciples' not judging others, He declares that they were as worthy of death as others who had died. The disciples' lack of qualifications, individually, to exercise capital judgment without proper governmental authority and responsibility was based on their own guilt.

In John 8:7, Jesus taught that the qualification for initiating capital judgment was one's own innocence. He said, "He that is without sin among you, let him first cast a stone at her." To exercise capital judgment against another for the breaking of God's command, one must himself be innocent of breaking any of God's commandments; that is, one must be sinless.

The woman taken in adultery should be stoned according to the Mosaic Law, but only Jesus was qualified to initiate judgment and to carry out the sentence for He was the only innocent one present. After each of those who had brought the woman for judgment had acknowledged their lack of the qualification—they had gone away one by one—Jesus said to the woman, "Neither do I condemn thee." Paraphrased, He said, "These others have realized that they are not qualified to judge you, and I, Who am qualified, choose not to judge you." That is the gospel, and that is the example for Christians, even in regard to abortionists.

Bray rejects the premise that only the innocent can initiate capital judgment because he rejects John 7:53—8:11 as being a legitimate part of Scripture.[4] Bray appeals to textual critics to support his rejection of the passage.[5] Those critics claim that while this text is "not authoritative; it is authentic." If this text is not a legitimate part of John's Gospel, how do textual critics know that it is authentic? If it is authentic, why is it not authoritative?

One textual critic, however, observed, "The argument which has always weighed most in its favor in modern times is its own internal character. The story itself has justly seemed to vouch for its own substantial truth, and the words in which it is clothed to harmonize with those of other Gospel narratives."[6] Textual criticism has done much to affirm the truth of the Word of God. No doctrine is developed from John 7:53—8:11 that is not substantiated fully and completely by other texts not subjected to doubt (for example, Luke 7:35–50).

The Text of Scripture

Westcott and Hort affirm the excellence of Scripture with this evaluation of the accuracy of the text which exists today:

The proportion of words virtually accepted on all hands as raised above doubt is very great, not less, on a rough computation, than seven eighths of the whole. The remaining eighth . . . formed in great part by changes of order and other comparative trivialities, constitutes the whole area of criticism . . . setting aside differences of orthography, the words in our opinion still subject to doubt only make up about one sixtieth of the whole New Testament.

In this second estimate the proportion of comparatively trivial variations is beyond measure larger than in the former; so that the amount of what can in any sense be called substantial variation is but a small fraction of the whole residuary variation, and can hardly form more than a thousandth part of the entire text.

Since there is reason to suspect that an exaggerated impression prevails as to the extent of possible textual corruption in the New Testament, which might seem to be confirmed by language used here and there in the following pages, we desire to make it clearly understood beforehand how much of the New Testament stands in no need of a textual critic's labours.

INTRODUCTION TO
THE NEW TESTAMENT
IN THE ORIGINAL GREEK, 2–3.

Bringing the entire weight of Scripture to bear on John 7:53—8:11, Jesus affirmed the Old Testament teaching that only innocent individuals could initiate capital punishment. The Old and New Testaments declare that there are no innocent individuals, therefore, no individual can initiate or carry out capital judgment. Jesus did affirm the law of God, but He also indicated that the law of love had superseded the laws of retaliation.

The woman could have been executed by one who is innocent, but she did not have to be. Love covered her nakedness and her sin. The import of John 7:53—8:11 is not the abolition of capital punishment, but that this text, along with numerous other New Testament references, declares who is qualified to initiate capital punishment for infractions of God's law. It is the one who is without sin.

Therefore, if it were righteous to execute those who are breaking God's law in committing abortion (and it is not), the only individual who could initiate that judgment would be the one who is sinless. This excludes this writer, Michael Bray, Paul Hill, and Michael Griffin.

It had always been the case that only the sinless could exercise capital judgment. In the Old Testament, no individual could stone another to death, only the covenant community could. Righteousness in the Old Testament was an issue of being part of the community of faith, the commonwealth of Israel. While sin was individual and while repentance was necessary, the establishment of righteousness—of sinlessness in the sight of God—was associated with being a member of the covenant community. Therefore the only one who could initiate capital judgment were the elders of Israel in conjunction with the people responsible for the one being judged.

In the New Testament, nothing has changed. The only one who can initiate capital judgment is one who is sinless before God. Now righteousness is not associated with the commonwealth of Israel, but it is associated with the house of David through Jesus Christ. One of the remarkable things about New Testament righteousness is that God judges one according to the head of the family in which he resides. Therefore, in Adam, no matter how good a man is, he is lost; in Christ, no matter how much a man struggles with sin, he is saved. The nature of New Testament righteousness has not changed from the Old Testament. It is seen both in our relationship to God—we love, worship, and obey Him—and in relationship to men—we love, forgive, and have mercy toward them.

Even if the text relating the woman taken in adultery is disregarded, the woman at the well in John 4 and the woman at Jesus' feet in Luke 7 show Christ's compassion toward women whom men have exploited, rather than being cherished and protected by them. No faith has done more to liberate women from second-class personhood than the Christian faith. The fact that feminists have distorted that liberation into a motive for sin does not change the fact that the Christian faith liberates women. The fact that God permits men to judge other men under the laws of men does not set aside the critical requirement of innocence in order to judge another guilty of a capital crime.

Pro-life advocates generally do not object to capital punishment, but they recognize that only the state can exercise such judgment, based upon the laws of the land. Pro-life advocates reject the right of vigilantes, who for their own private reasons choose to "execute" someone, to exercise capital judgment. When Christians reject the murdering of abortion providers, they do not reject capital punishment. They reject the idea that an individual can be judge, jury, and executioner.

Is This Pacifism?

Bray equates opposition to violence against abortion practitioners by vigilante actions with pacifism. This ignores a true understanding of pacifism and of the fact that society, particularly a democratic republic, has the right to ask Christians to eschew violence. To reject terrorism is not to embrace pacifism. The social contract that exists between the U.S. government and her citizens enables Christians to embrace peaceful debate and protest without compromising their convictions and without coercing others to accept their convictions about abortion.

13

GO TO THE
SPRING OF THE WATERS!

RETURNING HOME FROM witnessing the translation into heaven of his mentor, the prophet Elisha passed by Jericho. The town leaders told him that they had a problem: their water was contaminated and their land was barren (2 Kings 2:19–21). *Barren* referred to the animals and possibly the women having miscarriages. It is used in the same way in Hosea 9:14, "Give them, O LORD: what will thou give? give them a miscarrying womb and dry breasts." Miscarriage—spontaneous abortion—was always a judgment of God on a land and was always associated with sadness and grief.[1] The leaders of Jericho complained to Elisha about their dilemma. His response was instructive to them and to us as well.

Elisha did not institute a water-treatment program. He did not recommend a protest against the local water utility company. He did not place a picket around the water supply so that no one could get to the water. What he did do was to go to the spring of the water. He went to the source of the problem.

The people had told him of their problem, the bad water. Therefore, Elisha addressed his attention to the source of the water; he examined the spring from which the water flowed.

To solve the problem of abortion in America, we must follow Elisha's example. We should go to the source of abortion. Where is this source? Is it the abortion clinic or the infamous *Roe v. Wade* decision? Will the reversal of *Roe v. Wade* stop abortion in this country? The overturning of *Dred Scott* did not stop racism, and it is probable that the reversal of *Roe v. Wade* will not stop abortion. It would only move the conflict to a new arena. That is not necessarily bad, but it is reality.

How did abortion-on-demand become the law of the land? What prepared the way? What is the spring from which abortion flows? It is imperative to determine accurately the source of the problem, because with that determination we will define the solution. The spring from which abortion flows is not greed, guilt, or genuine interest in the welfare of others. The spring is the doctrine that man is the result of a mechanism, and therefore is not accountable to anyone for his choices. At first this assertion may seem strange, but on closer examination it will be clear that this is the case.

The Dogma of Evolution

With Charles Darwin's publication of *The Origin of Species*, the first formal step was taken in the development of a world-view that would inevitably lead to the evil of abortion. Darwin was more the popularizer of evolutionary theory than its originator; however, he codified the idea that man was the product, not of special creation with attendant accountability to his Creator, but of a long, tortuous process of mechanical factors without external control or influence, whereby the simple became more complex.

The twentieth century can be divided into three eras:

- **1900–1933.** The acceptance of evolution as the

dominant theory of origins, marked by the publication in 1933 of the Humanist Manifesto and signaled by the 1925 Scopes trial in Tennessee.

- **1933–1973.** The adoption of secular humanism as the dominant world-view in the United States marked by the publication of Humanist Manifesto II in 1971 and sealed by the Supreme Court's 1973 decision in *Roe v. Wade*.

- **1973–2000.** The approval of abortion as the cardinal tenet of the new secular faith, which has sacrificed a generation of children upon the altar of that faith.

The legal sideshow of the 1925 Scopes Monkey Trial demonstrated that evolution had been accepted as the dominant theory of origins. It was marked by the same duplicity as the later *Roe v. Wade* case. On May 5, 1925, in Robinson's Drugstore, Dayton, Tennessee, football coach John Thomas Scopes agreed to be the defendant in a case where he allegedly taught evolution, which was contrary to a new state law. Scopes later admitted he had never committed the offense for which he was tried. He had lied, saying that he had taught evolution to bring the case to court.[2]

Jane Doe, the pseudonym for Norma McCorvey, the plaintiff in *Roe v. Wade*, alleged that she became pregnant through rape. She has since admitted that she contrived the story to bring her case to court. Her pregnancy was actually the result of a casual affair.[3] While this does not affect the substance of the issues raised in these court decisions, it demonstrates the spirit of the principles in these cases.

Functional Atheism

The idea that man is not accountable to God is the foundation of "functional atheism." Many will argue philosophically for the existence of God but live as though He does not exist. Psalm 10 outlines the characteristics of the functional atheist:

- The functional atheist does not think about God (v. 4).

- The functional atheist is self-sufficient, believing that he needs nothing or no one outside of himself (v. 6).

- The functional atheist declares that God is not interested in what goes on upon the earth (v. 11).

- The functional atheist believes there is no accountability for what he does or does not do (v. 13).

Functional atheism is more dangerous and sinister than theoretical atheism because it disregards God as irrelevant.

Some would argue that evolutionary dogma—and it is a dogma unsupported by facts of science—is an established fact. Anyone who accepts the inerrant, inspired Word of God, the Bible, would disagree with that judgment. Immediately, some would label those who confess confidence in the Bible as "fundamentalist Neanderthals," ignorant and unlearned. But are they?

Philip E. Johnson, professor of law at the University of California at Berkeley, wrote *Darwin on Trial* in which he defends biblical creationism and challenges Darwinism. The *Houston Chronicle* reported that he had identified evolution as the biggest sacred cow in American life. "Johnson found the scientific evidence for evolution to be almost non-existent. . . . There were few fossils that could be interpreted as transitional forms from one species to another. . . . One [problem] was stasis, or a lack of evolutionary progress in millions of years, found among many species. That contradicted the continuous progression that evolution argued. . . . The acceptance of Darwin's answer 'was a delusion brought on by tremendous faith, a tremendous will to believe by the scientific community, which was mesmerized by the theory's great logical and imaginative appeal,' Johnson said." [4]

Evolutionary dogma is falling progressively into disrepute. Editor and writer Tom Bethell [5] wrote extensively on what he called "the most important academic debate of the 1960's," the debate that emasculated Darwin's theory of evolution. Bethell concluded, "it is beginning to look as though [Darwin] really discovered . . . nothing more than the Victorian propensity to believe in progress." [6]

Fossils provide the best scientific support for the creation model of origins because of the lack of "transitional forms" in the fossil record. "Phylectic gradualism" is the Darwinian dogma that everything gradually evolved from a simple to a complex form. This was never seen in the fossils, which are found in rock formations. If "phylectic gradualism" were true, the fossil record should show simpler forms underneath layers of successively complex forms. The fossils should show abundant transitional forms of one species "evolving" into another. Scientists at five leading natural history museums have confirmed:

- There are no transitional forms in the fossil record between classes, orders, and families.

- The earliest examples of all life forms in the fossil record appear structurally and functionally complete.

- Every major animal phylum is represented in the lowest rocks containing undisputed multicelled fossils.

This is exactly what the creation model of origins would have predicted, and it is the opposite of what is necessary for the fossil record to support an evolutionary model of origins.

In *Hermeneutics, Authority, and Canon,* John Woodbridge, in discussing biblical inerrancy, commented upon the problems with evolution. He said: "The changing theories of evolutionists are presently up for rigorous scrutiny. In a remarkable essay, 'Agnostic Evolutionists, The Taxonomic Case Against Darwin,' Tom Bethell writes: 'the theory of evolution has never been falsified. On the other hand, it is also surely true that positive evidence for evolution is very much weaker than most laymen imagine, and than many scientists want us to imagine. Perhaps, as Patterson says, that positive evidence is missing entirely." [7]

The evolutionary model of origins, like the creation model, cannot be reproduced in the laboratory. Therefore, whatever else it is—faith, fantasy, fable, or fiction—evolution is not scientific fact. Nonetheless, the facts of science —for example, the fossil record—are more intelligently explained by a creation model of origins than an evolutionary one.

In his book, *The Natural Sciences Know Nothing of Evolution,* A. E. Wilder-Smith, doctor of physical organic chemistry, stated, "Evolution . . . represents an attempt to explain the formation of the genetic code from the chemical components of DNA without the aid of a genetic concept [information] originating outside the molecules of the chromosomes. This is comparable to the assumption that the text of a book originates from the paper molecules on which the sentences appear, and not from any external source of information [external, that is, to the paper molecules]."[8] The only way a person can embrace the doctrines and dogma of evolution unreservedly is to ignore facts in favor of a religious faith that requires an inept or nonexistent God.

There are fewer "empirical fallacies" to the creationist's model of human origins than that of the evolutionists. It is no longer necessary for the Bible-believing advocate of the sanctity of human life to feel that his position is less defensible than that of the evolutionist. Most of all, it is unnecessary for the Christian to make any apology for the Word of God and its revelation of God the Creator. The facts fit revelation.

Evolution, Humanism, and Theological Liberalism

Darwinian evolution is the cornerstone doctrine of humanism and theological liberalism. Evolutionary dogma was the faith adopted by Darwin when he left seminary after denying his Christian faith. Evolution found its way into church life through liberal Christian theologians. One of the leading contenders for Christian liberalism was Harry Emerson Fosdick. One review of Baptist history said of Fosdick:

> Doubts about biblical infallibility plagued him.
> . . . Finally he read Andrew D. White's *History of the Warfare of Science with Theology in Christendom,* and that settled the matter for him. He no longer simply doubted, he positively opposed any concept of biblical inerrancy. Fosdick was fully convinced that scientific study had finally made the Bible truly intelligible. . . . Fosdick makes it sound as if the evolutionary approach is in fact God's best for true believers. . . . Fosdick lived in a 'new world' that had

outgrown . . . primitive beliefs. Modern man could not read the Bible and accept it as an ancient man would. Modern man simply knows better than to believe in these outdated scientific views. . . . According to Fosdick, Jesus recognized that there were outgrown elements in the Bible.[9]

Many modern Christians have embraced Fosdick's error, and with that embrace, they made abortion on demand possible.

Humanist Manifesto I, published in 1933, encapsulated Darwin's ideas and the implications of those ideas in its first, second, and fifth postulates:

- Religious humanists regard the universe as self-existing and not created.

- Humanism believes that man is a part of nature and that he emerged as the result of a continuous process.

- Humanism asserts that the nature of the universe depicted by modern science makes unacceptable any supernatural or cosmic guarantees of human value.

The 1933 *Humanist Manifesto II* is a short step from the 1983 *Pediatrics* article mentioned in chapter 2. Without the doctrine of evolution, humanism would have no foundation and abortion-on-demand would be impossible.

Evolutionary dogma has two corollaries:

- Man is the result of an impersonal mechanism: evolution. He is accountable only to himself. The circumstances in which he finds himself and the uncontrollable consequences of his actions, dictate his choices.

- Man has no intrinsic value. The utilitarian evaluation of what he can experience, produce, or contribute to society becomes the basis of determining the value of human life. Man, being only an animal, has no unique value above other animals.

If God is not the Creator, this argument goes, then He must not be the Judge. If He is not the Judge, there is no Judge, and man may do as he will.

The Importance of God as Creator

The battle for hearts and minds still revolves around the doctrine of origins. While no professing Christian would yield to an assertion that Jesus is not the Christ and is therefore not the Redeemer, many have yielded to the argument that He is not the Creator. The supplanting of God the Creator with a dispassionate mechanism such as evolution, is not only the root of abortion; it is also the root of many of the problems of faith that the church faces today.

In Jeremiah 33:20–21, 25–26, God confirms the relationship between His role as Creator and Redeemer. He states that if He did not create the order in the universe (Jer. 33:25) or if man is able to change His order (Jer. 33:20), then He, our Heavenly Father, cannot be the Redeemer of Israel. If He cannot be the Redeemer of Israel, He cannot be the Redeemer of Gentiles either. When the church yielded the Bible's position on creation, it unwittingly yielded its position on salvation as well.

Additional understanding of the importance of this connection between God the Creator and God the Redeemer is found in an analysis of the great prayers of the Bible. Hezekiah's prayer in 2 Kings 18, Jehoshaphat's prayer in 2 Chronicles 20, and the disciples prayer in Acts 4, all appeal to the God who is the Creator of all. One of the best-known verses on prayer in the Old Testament is

Jeremiah 33:3, "Call unto me, and I will answer thee, and show thee great and mighty things, which thou knowest not." The verse is preceded by the revelation of why Jeremiah could have confidence in God's capacity to answer prayers: God is the Creator.

The Psalmist pronounces the blessing of the man whose confidence is in the God of Jacob. The list of ten characteristics of the God of Jacob begins with "Which made heaven, and earth, the sea, and all that therein is" (Ps. 146:6). When John reveals the deity of Christ, he said, "All things were made by him; and without him was not any thing made that was made" (John 1:3).

The critical importance of the doctrine of creation is also demonstrated in that spiritual leaders who are to be followed must have a firm confidence in God as the Creator. Hebrews 13:7 gives the characteristics of those leaders who are worthy of being followed as:

- Belief in the existence of God.

- Confidence in God's being the creator and ruler.

- Knowledge that God is the provider and bestower of eternal life.

- Total confidence and faith in God personally (Jer. 17:5–8; Ps. 118:6–9).

- Assurance of the nature of God as being powerful, wise, and good.

Confidence in God's ability to redeem His people was based on their confidence in Him as the Creator. Confidence in God's capacity to answer prayer was also confidence in Him as Creator. Underlying the entire biblical revelation of God's eternal plan for man and the earth is the certainty that He created the world by "the breath of His mouth" (Ps. 33:6).

This is true today as well. While it is not necessary to believe that God created the heavens and the earth to be born again; it is necessary to have a strong confidence in Him as the Creator to battle successfully for Him in the conflicts that rage in this world. The vitality of one's spiritual life and the effectiveness of one's service for Christ will often be in proportion to the confidence one has in God as Creator. Before God's people could be lulled into capitulation about evolution, they had to surrender their confidence in God as the Creator. Evolution is the spring from which abortion flows.

What Should We Do?

After Elisha identified the spring of the water, he took a new cruse, placed salt in it, and cast the salt into the spring. This "healed" the waters, we are told in the Scripture. But what would it mean for us to throw salt into the evolutionary spring of abortion from a "new cruse"? The Lord Jesus Christ called His followers the salt of the earth. The apostle Paul, by revelation from Christ, said that when a man receives Christ as his personal savior, upon confessing and repenting of his sins, the follower of Christ becomes a new creature. If Christians are going to influence the moral climate of the nation and if they are going to effect real change in the abortion mills of America, it will be by being new creatures in Christ and by being the salt of the earth.

That's a good idea, but what does it mean in everyday life? Being a new creature is the result of a sovereign act of God Himself. The removal of the corruption of sin from a man's life is something only God can do. Therefore, only God can prepare a man to be a "new cruse." Once God has accomplished this miracle in a man's life, however, God places a significant responsibility upon the man himself to maintain the position of being a new cruse. This does not address the security of one's salvation; it addresses one's availability for service.

The new cruse position is maintained in a man's life by a clear conscience, which before God is maintained by confessing and repenting of any known sin in one's life. A clear conscience before man is maintained by the attempt to resolve any conflict between brothers or sisters in Christ or, for that matter, any person, so far as is possible. Then one lives one's life as an open book before the Lord and before the world.

Paul told Timothy he had only two weapons: his faith and his clear conscience (1 Tim. 1:18–19). A sure way to "shipwreck" your faith, Paul told Timothy, was to set aside a clear conscience. Courageousness for the Lord is only possible with a clear conscience. When one has a defiled conscience, he or she will always be fearful of exposure and will, therefore, be timid about the truth.

In 2 Timothy 2:21, Paul urged, "If a man therefore purge himself from these, he shall be a vessel unto honour, sanctified, and meet for the master's use, and prepared unto every good work." The preparation to be used of God, to apply the salt to the spring of evolution and therefore to heal the land of abortion, begins with purging oneself daily and regularly from the contamination of sin and of a defiled conscience.

The salt that we cast into the spring of evolution is the salt of Christ, the Creator and Lord of the universe and the only savior of mankind. It is the salt of the Word of God as the complete and completed revelation of God to man. It is the salt of man's accountability to God for his conduct. It is the salt of Christians with clear consciences confronting the world around them with the message, "Thou are the Christ, the Son of the living God" (Matt. 16:16). It is the salt of discipline that every believer must add to the promises of God (2 Pet. 1:5).

This is the only salt that will heal these springs from which flows the water of "naught," which makes the land "barren." The new cruse is a man or woman who is a new creature in Christ, always maintaining a clear conscience. The salt is the possibility of relationship with God through Christ, maintained through daily intimacy with Christ in prayer and meditation upon thw Word of God. This new cruse and this salt are the vehicles for the healing of the bitter waters of abortion. We must continue to rally. We must continue to march. We must, however, concentrate on being salt and new cruses.

To stop abortion, Christians themselves must be confident in God as the Creator, and they must pray and preach for the reestablishment of confidence in God as the Creator in society in general. They *will not* attempt to impose this belief upon others by coercion, intimidation, or terrorism.

Until man returns to the affirmation that God is the Creator, abortion will remain as a logical and acceptable alternative, no matter how aggressively Christians pursue either Operation Rescue or the approach that is recommended here. The proper place for activism by Christians is in the church and in the home to restore confidence in the God who created the heaven and the earth. God is more concerned with the church and her sins than He is with the human community and its sin.

Ultimately and finally, abortion will only be solved by a return to confidence in God as the Creator of all that is. With confidence in God as the Creator of man and with confidence that man is the special creation of a personal God, abortion-on-demand will no longer be acceptable public policy. This confidence will not result from threats or violence. It will not result from protest and picketing. It will result from preaching the truth under the power of God, the Holy Spirit.

14

A Modest Proposal

THERE IS LITTLE DOUBT that if Jesus walked into an abortion clinic in America today that all abortions would stop and all abortionists would repent or flee. In that Jesus sits at the right hand of the throne of God, the question is How do we get the spirit of Christ into the abortion question in America today? Jesus taught that His followers should overcome evil with good, which means Christians should overcome evil with God's character, because Jesus declared that only God is "good" (Matt. 19:17).

The apostle Paul taught Christians how to conduct themselves in the larger arena of society. J. B. Phillips translates Romans 12:21, "Don't allow yourself to be overpowered by evil. Take the offensive—overpower evil with good!" The ultimate proof of the Christian faith is demonstrated by how Christians deal with their enemies and how they deal with those who disagree with them. To love our friends and family is of little moment to the world. To love our enemies, however, shows that our lives are influenced by God's life.

Blessing Our Enemies

Christians must remember that it was while they were enemies of God that Jesus died for them. Therefore, Christians must show God's life to abortion providers and to those seeking abortion. We must find a way to do good for and to them. Blessing our enemies is not helping them accomplish their evil deeds, but it must show them our love in order to awaken God's love and God's law in their hearts (Romans 2).

To overcome the evil of abortion with good, we must first learn why a person wants an abortion and then meet the need that the person thinks an abortion will meet. Overcoming evil with good requires more than going to Wichita to picket an abortion clinic. It may require money to deliver the baby, clothes and a home in which to raise the baby, family acceptance, or help to find God's forgiveness for a moral failure.

How do we overcome evil with good when addressing abortion providers? This is difficult to know, but God will give us wisdom. One way to bless those who are involved in such evil is to pray *for* them and to pray *with* them if allowed.[1] It is contrary to human nature to pray for good to befall those whom we believe are doing evil. Yet, that is the divine nature, as the goodness of God leads men and women, boys and girls to repentance.

Several years ago, a man joined our church who had long hair and an earring. His job promoted the most offensive of all secular rock music groups. There are few things I personally disdain more on a man than long hair and earrings. There is nothing that I personally detest more than acid rock music. Yet, for God's own purposes, this man and I became friends.

As I began to encourage him to read the Bible and have a quiet time with the Lord, the subjects of music, hair, and earrings were never broached. Yet, very shortly, he stopped wearing the earring. Not long afterward, he came under conviction about his promotion of rock music and asked me to pray that he might find a different job.

Unknown to us, his employer was reconsidering its marketing strategy. In a few weeks, he was able to change jobs because he was fired by the record promotion company, along with 90 percent of the sales promotion force. Now he has a successful advertising business and is promoting businesses that are consistent with his Christian commitments.

The pro-life movement might be more effective if they prayed for good in the life of abortion providers rather than persecuting them. When Elijah proposed a demonstration project to determine whose God is the true God, he did not propose a shootout. He proposed competing prayer meetings.[2] If all abortion providers found it more profitable not to perform abortions, most of them would stop. If we pray for their good, it may be that they will find more profitable employment and stop doing abortions.

The San Francisco Experiment

There is a model for this kind of experiment. The *Southern Medical Journal* reported a "double blind" study of the efficacy of prayer in a coronary care unit. The research for the article, entitled "Positive Therapeutic Effects of Intercessory Prayer in a Coronary Care Unit Population," was conducted by the cardiology division of San Francisco General Medical Center and the department of medicine at the University of California, San Francisco. New admissions to the cardiac unit were randomly assigned to one of two groups: one would be prayed for and the other would not be. The random assignments were made with an effort to eliminate factors such as age, severity of illness, and other preexisting complications. The conclusion of the study was summarized in this statement, "The Intercessory Prayer group subsequently had a significantly lower severity score based on the hospital course after entry. . . . These data suggest that intercessory prayer to the Judeo-Christian God has a beneficial therapeutic effect in patients admitted to a CCU."[3]

None of the patients knew they were being prayed for, but those who were prayed for did better. The study correctly concludes "these data suggest . . ." Science rarely can say anything with certainty, particularly medical science, but the implications are there. Further studies can be done to confirm these results.

Proposed Experiment #1

I propose that we establish an experiment like Elijah's by dividing anti-abortion activists into four groups. Group One will be made up of those committed to confrontation and aggression. Members of this group will stand in front of an abortion clinic and shout at the people going into the clinic.[4] They will continue to carry placards that associate abortion with murder and with Nazi death camps. They will continue to threaten women going into abortion clinics with the judgment of God. Such a picture actually reminds me of the Baal prophets, who "leaped upon the altar. . . . And they cried aloud, and cut themselves" (1 Kings 18:26, 28).

Group Two will depend on the power of prayer. They will obtain the names and addresses of the employees of a particular abortion clinic. With the names of the children and the grandchildren of those employees, members of Group Two will pray that God will bless each employee.[5] They will pray that God will bless the husbands of the women employees with better jobs so that the wives will quit work. They could pray for the doctors to be offered better positions to take care of patients rather than killing babies. They could pray that the employees of the abortion clinic would be convicted of the sin in which they are involved. They could pray that those employees would repent of this sin and stop providing abortions.

This group would not pray that any harm will come to these employees or that they would be coerced into a change of heart.[6] They would pray that the goodness of

God will lead them to repentance (Rom. 2:1–4). As in any valid experiment, employees of the clinic will not know they are being prayed for and no demonstrations will take place at those clinics during the year.

Group Three could combine sidewalk counseling with prayer. This group would simply kneel in front of an abortion clinic and pray for those going in and those doing the abortions. They would not say anything to anyone, but speak only to God. This group would require a considerable degree of Christian maturity not to be sanctimonious about long, public prayers, like the Pharisees. Yet God would bless and honor the humble, brokenhearted spirit that such a demonstration would reflect if done properly.

Group Four could do sidewalk counseling exactly as it has been done in many places all over the country. Many Christians are brokenhearted over the evils of abortions: babies' being killed, women being assaulted, and men and women profiting from evil. These brokenhearted Christians could gather at the abortion clinics. They could peaceably assemble and quietly go about the business of offering alternatives to women who want them. There would be no shouting or grotesque signs of mutilated babies. There would simply be the loving and gentle offer of help. Any signs that did exist would be affirming life, not dramatizing death. Any materials distributed would be offering alternatives, not adding to the guilt and pain of hurting men and women by accusing them of Nazi-like crimes.

This experiment would continue for one year. At the end of that time, an assessment could be made as to whether God is able to change the heart of abortionists like He changed the heart of my friend. I am confident that the results would demonstrate the power of prayer, even in the face of abortion. This experiment would be much easier to evaluate than the San Francisco experiment. When abortion clinics began to close, not because the employees were afraid to go to work, but because they had found more fulfilling and profitable work, the power of prayer over persecution would be demonstrated. The experiment also has the benefit of Christians being able to say to their God: We hate what is going on in those clinics, but we know that You hate it, too. What do You want to do about this?

A similar experiment could be undertaken for women who are seeking abortions. It would be more difficult to design and enlist participants, but many women who have one abortion have other abortions. If a means for identifying the women seeking abortions could be devised, one-year, two-year, and three-year followups could be done to see if the pattern had been changed more effectively by prayer or confrontation.

Paul's counsel not to use evil methods, that is, illegal, criminal, or ungodly methods, to oppose evil (Rom. 12:17–20) is a clear application of our Lord's words in Matthew 5:44–48, where Jesus declared that to be perfect as His Father is perfect, man must love and do good for his enemies. What is wrong with this approach? Simply, most Christians are reluctant to let the results be taken out of their hands. Most Christians are driven by a desire to succeed. Yet the only time faith can be exercised—the only time men and women can be courageous for the Lord—is when they live by biblical principles and by the spirit of Christ, even when they don't know how it will turn out. When Christians leave the results in God's hands, they can remain faithful to God's commandments and to His character.

Regrets, Yes—Doubts, No

Several years ago, a fellow physician was indicted for sexual molesting a minor. This man had been a neighbor and friend when he was married, but when he divorced his wife and entered a homosexual lifestyle, we no longer saw one another socially. When his indictment became public knowledge, I called him and said, "I hate what you are and I hate what you do, but you are my friend and I want to help if I can."

As I talked with him, my wife and children gathered around, listening to the conversation and praying for wisdom. My friend said, "I'm not asking for anyone to excuse what I have done, but I do need forgiveness." I told him, "The only hope I have to offer you is Jesus Christ, and if you would like to meet, I will still be your friend." At this point, he said, "I can't make any guarantees or promises, but I need a friend." I assured him that there were no strings attached to my offer to be his friend in his crisis.

We began to meet. Many criticized me for publicly eating with an accused child molester and, ultimately, a convicted felon. Some Christians suggested that I was supporting homosexuality by being this man's friend openly. We met for four to six hours a week for six months. I invited him to my home. My children received him as they prayed for him. My wife prepared meals for him and, in times of desperate, self-destructive depression, provided hope with her love and care.

After six months, this man, who had violated the trust of his profession, his community, and himself, was able to answer the question that we had discussed for hours, Can God forgive me? When he was able to see that Christ's love and mercy were greater than sin, even his sin, he humbly and quietly walked down the aisle of a church giving his heart to the Lord Jesus Christ.

In the months that followed his conversion, my friend gave public testimony of his faith in Christ. He withdrew from all relationships with sodomy. He discovered that true intimacy, true love, is found in personal relationship with Christ, not in perversion. Two months after his salvation experience, my friend developed a cough and discovered that he was HIV positive. He deteriorated rapidly and died less than six months later. My wife and I visited in his home for hours during his final illness. We prayed with him and for him. We read the Word of God to him. We taught him how to memorize the Bible. We held his hands as he died.

At his funeral, attended by more than six hundred people, many of them not Christians, my friend's testimony influenced many. Another physician friend read the Scriptures that our friend had memorized before his death. As I closed his memorial service, I quoted the words of Eric Liddell, the Scottish runner whose life was portrayed in the movie *Chariots of Fire*. I reminded the congregation of Liddell's words as he watched the finals of the 100 meters at the Olympics. Except for his convictions that he should not race on the Lord's Day, most believed that Liddell would have won the 100 meters finals. As he watched the beginning of the race, Liddell's trainer and friend leaned over and asked, "Any regrets?"

Had I written the screenplay, I would have put the following words into Liddell's mouth, "Oh, no! Absolutely not." In doing so, I would have missed the most profound statement in the dramatization of Liddell's life. Liddell looked at his friend and said, "Yes, but no doubts." He had regrets; he would have loved to run that race, but he had no doubts about God's will in the matter.

As my friend's memorial service came to a close, I said, "When our friend stood before the throne of Almighty God last Thursday, and as the Lord Jesus Christ stepped down from that throne and put His arms around our friend, saying, 'Father, this is one of Mine,' our dear, precious friend had many regrets about his life, as I have many about mine, but he had no doubts of his acceptance, of his forgiveness, and of his Lord."

The Victory of the Cross

If pro-life advocates are going to rescue babies, mothers, and abortion providers, they are going to have to risk failure,

176

misunderstanding, and rejection. In so risking, they will perhaps for the first time be exercising courage and faith in Christ. The biblical principle underlying Romans 12:17–21 is this: God does not employ evil in resisting evil. The word translated *evil* in Romans 12:21 means "morally wrong, wicked; contrary to law, either divine or human, crime." Paul really declares, Don't commit a crime to resist a crime. When Christians oppose abortion with methods which are consistent with the Word of God and with the character of Christ, they may have regrets that they did not stop abortion-on-demand but they will have no doubts that they have honored God.

In the case of Operation Rescue, a crime is committed against the human law to stop a crime against the divine law. According to the New Testament, Christians should not do that except in very narrow circumstances, which do not presently exist in the United States. According to Kansas law, abortion is legal in Dr. Tiller's Wichita clinic, but trespass is illegal. Paul says, "Exercise faith, not force." Does God's legislation against evil allow us to set aside human legislation? Romans 12 exclaims, "No!"

The single instance where God's legislation supersedes man's legislation and *allows,* indeed *requires,* the unilateral setting aside of man's legislation via civil disobedience, is when the law requires evil to be done. Even then evil is not resisted by committing another crime; it is only resisted by the refusal to obey the coercive law that is itself a crime against God's justice.

In many ways, the abortion mill in America is directly traceable, not to the church's failure to use force, but to the church's failure to be the redemptive body that God designed it to be. The church has not taught doctrine to her people. The church has yielded the field on the doctrine of creation to evolutionists, allowing abortion to be established in America.

Earlier this century, the church rejected God's doctrine of separation and substituted seduction as a means of trying to win the world to Christ. Unfortunately, all that the church succeeded in doing was attracting the world into the church without transforming it. Much of the frenetic energy expended by the church to get people to attend church today can be traced to that compromise. The catastrophe of abortion is the price paid for the church's compromise on holiness, righteousness, and truth. This catastrophe will not be eliminated by punishing the world for the church's failure.

For anti-abortionists to neglect the preaching of the Cross, and, therefore, of redemption only plays into the hands of the enemy. If Christians really want to change the laws of the land, if they really want to stop abortion in America, it will require a tremendous pro-life commitment on the part of all anti-abortionists.

Christians will need to relinquish many of the resources now being expended upon religious activities, such as the building of bigger and bigger buildings and presenting bigger and bigger programs, all of which often conceal a smaller and smaller commitment to faith. Those resources will need to be reallocated to the financial and emotional support of unwed mothers, the medical support of problem pregnancies, the spiritual and emotional support of children brought into crisis-ridden homes, and the physical relief of the pressures of child rearing on emotionally crippled parents. Christians will have to spend time and money on counseling services for those who are seeking abortions and who are willing to listen to alternatives. Those counseling services should also be available to women after having had abortions.

It is not enough for Christian leaders simply to declare their rejection of violence in the pro-life movement, they must address the arguments of those who advocate violence.

It is not enough for anti-abortionists to posture themselves in decrying the evil of abortion without "putting their money where their mouth is." James 2:14–16 and 1 John 3:16–17 are biblical statements of this principle. James 2:14–16 states, "What doth it profit, my brethren, though a man say he hath faith, and have not works? can faith save him? If a brother or sister be naked, and destitute of daily food, And one of you say unto them, Depart in peace, be ye warmed and filled; notwithstanding ye give them not those things which are needful to the body; what doth it profit?"

To tell men and women ensnared in sin that there is a way out is not an honest Christian position if you are unwilling for God to use you to provide the resources necessary for their deliverance.[7] First John 3:16–17 states, "Hereby perceive we the love of God, because he laid down his life for us: and we ought to lay down our lives for the brethren. But whoso hath this world's good, and seeth his brother have need, and shutteth up his bowels of compassion from him, how dwelleth the love of God in him?"

It is not enough to recognize the error of abortion; it is not enough to oppose abortion. It is not enough to demonstrate against abortion. To be righteous, Christians must give themselves to others. There is no room here for Bray's "role distinction" through which he attempts to explain why Christ's method for reaching others should not be our method. Christians are to respond to evil in the lives of others, just like Jesus did, that is, by laying down their lives for them.

There is no "doctrine of progress" to justify Bray's idea that, although Jesus was self-sacrificing, Christians today should sacrifice others. Christians are to sacrifice themselves, not others. Christians, like their Savior, are to become poor that others might be made rich through their poverty.

Christians must balance physical and social concerns with the redemptive message of the gospel, lest their efforts degenerate into a twenty-first-century repetition of the error of the twentieth-century Social Gospel. In balance with truth and salvation, concern for the physical needs of men and women is a legitimate part of the gospel.

Nothing is so absent from the pro-life movement as is brokenheartedness. It is one thing to know that abortion is wrong. It is another to weep for those who believe the only hope they have is abortion. It is one thing to know that capital punishment is right and just; it is another to weep for those whose choices and life circumstances have brought them to death row. Few activities are as Christlike as the tear-stained eyes of those who weep over the wickedness of others.

Just after denouncing the evil of Pharisaism in Matthew 23, Jesus looked over religious Jerusalem and wept. He wept over the pain and sin of God's creation. The prophets were characterized by a strong, bold message, but they also were brokenhearted over the sin of the very people whose judgment they foretold. The Book of Jonah tells us that God was displeased because Jonah wanted Him to destroy Ninevah. Jeremiah prayed, "Oh that my head were waters, and mine eyes a fountain of tears, that I might weep day and night for the slain of the daughter of my people!" (Jer. 9:1).

The essence of Pharisaism is indifference to the pain of others. The Book of Hebrews declares that the high priest of Israel could have compassion upon others because of his own sin. Compassion is not compromise; it is the consistent application of God's commandments through convictions, not only to our own lives, but also in our dealings with others. The Bible states, "For every high priest . . . can have compassion on the ignorant, and on them that are out of the way; for that he himself also is compassed with infirmity" (Heb. 5:1–2). Compassion for others, even others who are committing what we believe is the worst sin on the earth, is the necessary response to our understanding of our own sin. Compassion will cause us to bring Christ's spirit to the failures of others.

Pro-life advocates must share the heartache of those who are seeking abortion. They must share the shame of those who are staffing abortion clinics. To reflect the character of Christ, they must see that those who are actually doing the abortions are victims, also.

Victim status does not excuse anyone from the moral consequences of wrong choices, but it does remove others as objects of physical attack and assault by Christians. Seeing abortion providers and those seeking abortions as victims, in the same way that the child who is being aborted is a victim, enables Christians to recognize that we are not fighting against flesh and blood. Abortionists are not the enemy; they are another victim of our enemy, who is the god of this age, Lucifer (see 2 Corinthians 4).

Opposition to abortion is spiritual warfare. It cannot be fought with secular weapons; it must be fought with spiritual ones. Both 2 Corinthians 10 and Ephesians 6 give insight and understanding about how to wage spiritual warfare.[8] That battle will be waged with truth, tears, and time spent alone with God interceding for those who are sinning.

If success is the goal of the pro-life anti-abortion movement, then the reality is that what has been being done hasn't worked. It may have satisfied the egos of those who have become most radical. It may have provided some war stories for after-church fellowship meetings, but like so many of the efforts of contemporary Christianity, it has not worked. Perhaps it is time to discover, through the Bible and the spirit of Christ, God's methods for dealing with evil.

Public Opinion Unchanged

"The fact is . . . that after the grueling Wichita standoff, public opinion on abortion did not change, according to a Gallup poll. The number favoring fully legal abortion held at 33 percent; those favoring a complete ban on abortion stayed at 14 percent; and those favoring legal abortion, but only in certain cases, held at 49 percent. More damaging to Operation Rescue were the data that showed that, of Americans who were aware of OR's activities, only 15 percent approved of its tactics."9

Killing abortionists is not only wrong, it is not even effective. The god of this world delights in violence and in force. Until the end of this age, when Christ shall judge all men, the god of this age wins whenever violence or force is employed in a religious effort, because one of the ways in which Satan is worshiped is in resorting to his tactics of coercion and terrorism.

Nothing was so characteristic of the Pharisees and perhaps nothing is so characteristic of religious fundamentalism today as sanctimonious indifference to the pain of others. The religious will focus upon the error of those who commit sin. The religious will focus on how those in sin contradict the law of God. The religious will want to "punish" those who "break" God's law.

The righteous will hate sin. The righteous will hate the sin of those who are in error. Because the righteous will confess with Paul, "we also are men of like passion" (Acts 14:15), their identification with others will enable them to empathize with those who compromise. Like the righteous one, Jesus Christ, the righteous today will feel the pain of those who have failed and who are failing. The righteous will not excuse the sin of others, but the righteous will weep for their pain. The righteous will be more concerned for rescuing those who have failed than for simply judging them. The righteous will be more preoccupied with redemption than with retribution.[10]

There is no question that the Pharisees would find it right to put a person to death for the breaking of the law of God, as they interpreted that law (see Acts 6). There is no question that a righteous man, and particularly the righteous man, Jesus Christ, would never consider it righteous to put one to death in this life for breaking God's law.

15

WHAT WILL CHRIST
HAVE US DO?

IF YOU ARE ASKING me whether my people should go out and possibly be killed, I don't know, I just don't know." So spoke the pastor of a small congregation in the movie *High Noon*. The indecisiveness of this character was one of the first attempts by Hollywood to belittle ministers of the gospel and other Christians. Yet, it does point out the fact that Christians often seem not to know what to do. One of the questions with which some Christians struggle is, Is it better to do nothing for fear of doing the wrong thing? Is it better to do the wrong thing in opposing evil, than to do nothing about evil? Although the end does not justify the means, indifference toward evil is not a proper response for believers. Merely recognizing that a particular person's action is wrong does not excuse a Christian from doing what is right.

Passion for Righteousness

It is possible in certain circumstances to do the wrong thing for the right reason and, because of the purity of one's heart and motive, not incur the judgment of God. Rahab and Moses illustrate this principle. Rahab lied, but her motive was such that she is remembered for helping to further God's redemptive plan and not for the sin of lying. Moses killed a man and there were temporal consequences in his life (forty years in the wilderness). Yet, God did not condemn Moses for this act. God does not commend those who do the wrong thing for the right reason, but neither does it appear that He condemns them. Neither Rahab nor Moses, however, provide an excuse for Christians to ignore God's commandments concerning homicide and honesty.

Nevertheless, it is possible to do the right thing for the wrong reason and incur the judgment of God because of a wrong motive. Ananias and Sapphira gave part of all that they had to the Lord. Because they did it to gain favor with the church and because they pretended to give everything to the church, God condemned them.

Yet, God's greatest condemnation for believers is reserved for the indifferent. Passivity and complacency are more objectionable to God than error.[1] It is because of passivity and complacency that the Laodicean church will be spewed out of the mouth of God (Rev. 3:15ff). God created man to be enthusiastic, to care about the things that He cares about. God desires that our lives be filled with a passion for the things that He loves and for the things He wills.

Paul desired this passion for all believers. He wrote the Ephesian Christians, "That you may really come to know—practically, through experience for yourselves—the love of Christ, which far surpasses mere knowledge (without experience); that you may be filled through all your being unto all the fullness of God—that is may have the richest measure of the divine Presence and become a body wholly filled and flooded with God Himself" (Eph. 3:19, AMP). It is the passion of the one "filled and flooded with God Himself"—under the control and direction of God, the Holy Spirit—who will declare to others, Lead, follow, or get out of the way!

Error should never be institutionalized, but neither should mediocrity. Operation Rescue participants have commendable passion, but they need to be corrected for their error. The church does not have to judge those who attack abortion providers, the state has been ordained of God to do that, but the church must make certain that it does not become a haven for those who espouse or practice violence.

Pharisaism is characterized principally by the disjunction between words and works, and it is in this disjunction that men deny God. Speaking of the Cretans, Paul told Titus: "They profess that they know God; but in works they deny Him" (Titus 1:16). Those who take comfort in correct words, even in regard to Operation Rescue, must look to their own works lest they fall into the error of the Cretans: pretending to love God, but exposing their pretense by their actions.

Remember, James said, that to know what is right and to do nothing about it is sin (James 4:17). The essential characteristic of the Pharisees was understanding what was right and doing nothing about it (Matthew 23). This is often the position of conservative Christians today. Determined to do nothing themselves, they complain about and condemn those who do.

In Romans, Paul examines the error of the Jews, but he commends their passion in Romans 10. A man without passion is a man without a purpose for life. A man without a purpose for life is a man without God, for God has purpose for the life of every man. Paul also told Titus: "Looking for that blessed hope, and the glorious appearing of the Great God and our Savior Jesus Christ; Who gave Himself for us, that He might redeem us from all iniquity, and purify unto Himself a peculiar people, zealous of good works" (Titus 2:13–14). God is looking for a people "zealous of good work," not a people driven by "violent zeal."

Peter did the wrong thing in the Garden of Gethsemane —he cut off a man's ear. With proper instruction, however, his zeal enabled him to be one of the men used of God in founding the New Testament church. There are many who can enumerate the reasons why Peter's action was wrong; there are few who have been used of God as was Peter. Without Peter's passion, which had him both jumping out of a boat and cutting off another's ear, he would have been useless to God. To become useful, even with his passion, Peter had to be submissive to the word, will, and way of God.

Never let it be said that those who object to Operation Rescue's methods do not admire their passion and their commitment! Never let it be said that those who object to Operation Rescue's methods wish to comfort those who passively dishonor God by doing nothing about the evil of abortion, all the while criticizing those who are about the kingdom of God's business as best they understand that business. It is often easier to moderate the teachable person, who is doing the wrong thing, than it is to overcome the immobility of the passive person who understands what is right and does nothing about it.

The physical law of inertia illustrates this spiritual principle. The law states that a body in motion tends to stay in motion, and a body at rest tends to stay at rest until acted upon by another force. The force required to alter the course and/or the speed of a body in motion is often less than that required to initiate motion in a similar body at rest.

All who are involved in God's kingdom's work must remain teachable and sensitive to God—open to the Lord, and possibly, His redirection. Abraham placed Isaac upon the altar at God's command. As he obeyed, he continued to listen for instructions. If he had not, Israel would have bled to death on Mount Moriah. Because Abraham was attentive to God, even while obeying Him, he was greatly used of

God. To be useful to and to be used of God, those who love God must continue to listen to Him, even as they serve Him. To cease to listen to God or to cease to listen to the cautions of His people is to cease to serve God effectively and to begin to serve oneself or one's course.

Therefore, in that we reject the methods of Operation Rescue and of the violent anti-abortionists, what shall we then do? We have already discussed a prayer vigil. This is imperative and would bring about a dramatic change in the abortion industry in America. But, there is mroe.

A Picture of Joey

Five years ago, a patient asked if I would see her pregnant daughter. I am not an obstetrician, but I told her I would help with her daughter's prenatal care; her daughter suffered with severe juvenile diabetes. Every obstetrician she had seen had told her that she would have to have an abortion. When I saw her, she expressed a desperate desire to give birth to her baby. As abortion was not an option to me, no matter what the circumstances, I offered my help.

When Joey was born, he had multiple abnormalities. He had no ears and his eyes were deformed. He had to have a permanent tracheotomy because of an abnormality of his trachea. Every time Joey breathed he spewed mucous on whomever was holding him.

Several years before Joey was born, I had met a family with the four handsomest children I have ever seen. When the oldest child turned nine, he asked to spend time with me. We began to meet, and I taught him how to have a quiet time, how to memorize Scripture, and how to share his faith. In the ensuing years, as we have continued to meet, this young man has become one of the most precious gifts that God has given me. He travels with our ministry team and is a great encouragement to all of us.

I first held Joey when he was four months old, I looked at his little deformed body and wiped the mucous from my face, sprayed from his tracheotomy with his every breath. As I held Joey, the Lord brought my other young friend to mind and reminded me of how handsome and winsome he is. In my spirit, the Lord said, "If you cannot love Joey as you love John [not his real name], don't ever tell me you are pro-life."

Tears ran down my face as I held Joey close to my heart and prayed God's blessing upon him. A picture of Joey sits on my desk to remind me to pray for him. My entire family knows and loves Joey. He was in my office the day before I wrote this chapter, and as he ran down the hall, giving instructions to his proud mother and father, I remembered that he was never supposed to be able to walk. He was never supposed to be able to talk. Joey brings light and brightness to every room he enters. One who has never been able to know and love a Joey will never completely know how deeply God loves us.

According to the *Pediatrics Journal* article quoted earlier in chapter 2, Joey did not have a chance to become much of a human being. According to God, he is a great human being. Joey has some hard days ahead of him as he gets older, but God has given some of us a special gift. He has given us the opportunity to be Joey's friend and to help him discover Jesus Christ as his friend. His grandmother is gone now, but her prayers are still being answered as Joey continues to grow in favor with God and man.

Joey's story and his life reminds me about what this entire pro-life struggle is all about. It is about letting little babies grow up. It is about men not deciding that they know what is best for others. It is about men not deciding that not being born with a deformity or some other problem is better than being born and learning to love and be loved while struggling with those problems. The challenge of Joey's story leaves us with the question, "What should we then do?"

Seven Ways Christians Can Affirm Life

The First Way: Respecting All Persons

The Bible often instructs believers not to "respect persons" (for example, Deut. 1:17). This really means that we should not judge that some people are better than others because of their wealth and power, or because they are members of our circle of friends. We should not judge that some are inferior to others for whatever reason. Christian love requires us to treat others mercifully and lovingly, even if they are different from us. The "respecter of persons" enters into the same judgment of the value of life as the abortionist and becomes his blood brother.

The Second Way: Rejecting Racism

Affirming all human life as valuable means that all racism is a reproach to God. Christians must know and declare that the racist is blood brother to the abortionist, both attempt to deny the dignity of life to another whom they judge as unworthy of life. Just as *Dred Scott* was eventually overturned because it was evil, so *Roe v. Wade* and *Doe v. Bolton* will be overturned because they are evil. Yet with the prominent vestiges of racism remaining in the Christian church today, with its tacit embracing of the errors of *Dred Scott*, the church's opposition to *Roe v. Wade* sometimes rings hollow to those who recognize the contradiction.[2]

The Third Way: Rejecting Gossip

Christians can affirm that all human life is precious to God by rejecting gossip, both in not doing it and in not receiving it. The Proverbs declare that "life and death are in the power of the tongue" (Prov. 18:21). Ephesians 4:28 declares that grace can be ministered by the tongue of man. James declares that the tongue can be set on fire with the fire of hell (James 3:6). Jesus associated calling a man a fool with the taking of his life (Matt. 5:21–22).

Like the abortionist, who steals the life of a child, and like the racist, who steals the life of a man by denying him dignity, the gossip attempts to steal the life of another with lies or half-truths. The gossip is blood brother to the abortionist, and the church will not have a strong testimony as it rails against abortion and raises another generation of gossips.

The Fourth Way: Opposing Child Abuse

The church must overcome evil by allowing no child to be abused without penalty. It is not enough for Christians to love their own children, they must learn to love all children. In Titus 2:4, the King James Version reads, "love their children"; the Greek text says, "love children." Evil must be overcome by allowing no child to go hungry. Love is not an idea; it is an act (James 2:14–16). Evil must be overcome by allowing no child to be homeless (Isa. 58:7). Evil must be overcome by allowing no pregnant woman to be neglected—physically, medically, emotionally, or spiritually (Matt. 25:34–46). This evil can be overcome initially by the church rejecting the subtle anti-children attitudes present among many Christians.

The Fifth Way: Creating Crisis Pregnancy Centers

Christians must overcome evil with good by creating crisis pregnancy centers, ministering not only to women considering an abortion, but to any woman whose pregnancy places stress on the family, emotionally or financially. The spirit and attitude of these clinics must not be, You have a problem, and I have the answer. It must be, We're in this together.

Christians must affirm all human life as precious to God by putting the welfare of another's life above our personal pleasure (Jer. 22:15ff). This means that if the church building program consumes all of the funds that could be spent on the support of pregnant women, the church stands as blood brother to the abortionist (Hos. 8:14).

The Sixth Way: Rejecting Violence

Christians can overcome evil with good by consistently and courageously rejecting violence against anyone in the name of Christ. At dinner one evening, this book was being discussed by my family and a few friends. As we discussed what a Christlike response to anti-abortion violence would be, my son said, "Dad, it may be that the time is coming when the godly thing would be for Christians to offer protection to abortionists." My son hates abortion and has no sympathies with abortion providers. The disturbing reality to me is that he may be right.

The Seventh Way: Bringing the Spirit of Christ to the Abortion Clinic

Earlier it was said that if Christ walked into an abortion clinic, all abortions would stop. How do we bring the spirit of Christ to the abortion clinic? We do it through conviction, compassion, confrontation, and comfort. Conviction means that we affirm that all abortions, for any reason and at any time, are wrong. Yet, we know that the sin of abortion is no more or less objectionable in the sight of God than other sins more commonly found in the church. Compassion means that our heart aches for the consequences of others' failures. We love others, not by approving of their sin, but by caring for them in their sin. Confrontation means that we gently and kindly tell others the undiluted truth about God's judgment of what they are doing. Yet, we do it in a way that lets them know that we have areas in which we have failed or are failing ourselves. Comfort means that we offer ourselves—not just our resources, but ourselves—to those who are hurting because they have failed. We comfort them with the comfort wherewith we have been comforted (2 Cor. 2:4). It is in this way that the spirit of Christ is brought to the abortion issue. There is no compromise, but neither is there condemnation.

Changing Hearts

Christians must agitate against evil. They must legislate against evil, especially the evil of abortion. They must also recognize, however, that, in the end, demonstrations against something will have little impact, while demonstrations of the compassion, love, and care of the Lord Jesus Christ will move mountains (1 John 3:15–18). The church must be the salt of the kingdom of God and the light of the Lord Jesus Christ on this earth, in this place, at this time for all children, born and unborn. Christians must maintain themselves as "new cruses" continually, constantly, consistently.

The church must bring the *conviction* of the value that God places on all human life and the *compassion* that Christ has for all children to bear upon current events with such passion that all men will be warned that they dare not defile the womb of another woman. Christians must affirm man's accountability to a holy creator God—an accountability that will bring a day of judgment, a day of terror, for all who transgress the commandments of God. The church must reestablish confidence in God as the Creator of man, the awe-inspiring Creator, who is a loving God whose terrible wrath in judgment had the apostle Paul tremble as he spoke the words, "knowing the terror of the Lord we persuade men" (2 Cor. 5:11).

Christians must affirm to every man, woman, and child that without the redemptive power of the blood of Christ3 hell awaits all respecters of persons, all racists, and all gossips, along with liars, murderers, adulterers, and abortionists. Christians must affirm that terror awaits those whose hands drip with the blood of innocent babies—creations of Almighty God. That terror will cause the hair to turn ashen, the breath to cease, the blood in the veins to boil, and the lips to be paralyzed in the cry of anguish from the presence of an almighty and holy Creator God, Who says, "It is impossible but that offenses will come; but woe unto him, through whom they come! It were better for him that a millstone were hanged about his neck, and he cast into the sea, than that he should offend one of these little ones" (Luke 17:1–2).

Christians must raise society's consciousness of the evil of abortion by agitating against *Roe v. Wade*. This must, however, be done within the constraints of submission to authority in our society. No society is strengthened by efforts to oppose wrong that actually undermine the nation's security and stability.

With all of these efforts, however, it is unlikely that much effective change will be accomplished. Long-term change in public policy, with an attendant change in personal conduct, will not be accomplished by this agitation. The Civil Rights movement has never completely accomplished its goals because most goals require a change of the heart, which cannot be effected by agitation. The nonviolent, noninflammatory agitation should continue, but its potential for success is limited. I do not believe that agitation efforts will ultimately effect long-term change in public policy.

Pro-life Is Costly

Liberals are often right when they say conservative Christians seem more committed to demanding that babies be protected *en utero* than in providing care and protection for them once they are born. It is expensive to be pro-life rather than simply being anti-abortion. It is expensive both in money and in time. It is expensive in emotions when one realizes that pro-life means that you stand against racism as much as against abortion.

Also, being pro-life is expensive, as sacred cows, at whose altars we have worshiped for years, are brought down. The Word of God affirms that it is by mercy and truth that iniquity is purged. In regard to sexual sins, the church is often big on truth, because that can simply be preached on Sunday morning by a "hired hand," and short on mercy, because that requires participation on Monday morning by the occupants of the pew and pulpit. Exercising a biblical balance of mercy and truth in regard to sexual sins often causes Christians to have to deal with their own struggles, vulnerabilities, or failures, none of which is comfortable.

Christians cannot have it both ways. Either we compassionately embrace those who have failed morally and are pregnant out of wedlock, or we continue to push the abortion mills to capacity in America. As previously reported, one major "Christian" university suspended a student who was pregnant. The administration did not want the student to have an abortion. Yet, their decision could have encouraged just that had the student's convictions been weaker.

There is a balance. We must not suggest that there are no consequences to sexual sins. A person who rebelliously lives in habitual sin must be disciplined by the church, part of which is exclusion from fellowship, the purpose of which is redemption and restoration. Yet, we do not want to reward those who secretly commit abortion and punish those who refuse to kill God's creation in the womb.

The only true hope to end abortion in America is revival. This is not an appeal for a revival of religion; it is an appeal for the revival of biblical faith. That revival is not directed toward the world; it is directed toward the church.

Abortion will not be stopped by changing the opinions of the courts about whether a baby in the womb is a baby; abortion will be stopped by those who profess to be Christians obeying God, exalting His Word, and exalting His Son.

The reason the Bible cannot be read in public schools is not because of wicked public education; it is because of the weakness of Christians and of their churches. The reason we have abortion on demand in this nation is not because of the wickedness of the Congress and Supreme Court; it is because of the weakness of Christians and, therefore, the weakness of the church.

The church must also repent of her own antagonism to children. The church has subtly participated in an antichild mentality. Large families must not be subjected to ridicule in our churches. Couples that have children close together must not be the focus of crude jokes. The church must reject the philosophy that children are a burden.

Family Circle, a popular cartoon in the daily newspaper, recently showed the father worrying over bills. He said to his wife, "Has it ever occurred to you how rich we would be if we did not have four children and three dogs?" His wife responded, "It has occurred to me how poor we would be." The church must stop viewing children as financial pressures and delight in them as the rich heritage of the Lord. We must be sensitive to the barren couples in our churches, but we must also be sensitive to encourage those who have been blessed of the Lord with a "quiver full of children."

Christians must also reevaluate their acceptance of the right and the power to control the number of children and when they will have children. All believers must evaluate birth control for themselves. However, we must recognize that we have bought into the secular humanist agenda of the world with our flippant acceptance of contraceptives, tubal ligations, and vasectomies. It may be that God wants us to reevaluate how these methodologies are reflecting negative attitudes toward children.

There are legal and excellent means available today to oppose abortion effectively in the courts of America. Many women are being injured in abortion clinics. Medical malpractice litigation is pursued normally for economic reasons and/or because of bitterness on the part of patients. The holding of someone financially and legally liable for failure to perform a miracle or for being human and making a mistake is contrary to the biblical message, but in the case of injuries due to abortion, malpractice litigation would be legitimate.

While the church is regaining the ground she has relinquished through fear, slothfulness, and lust, she must protest the abuses of God's creation in society today. The church must protest loudly, publicly, and persistently, but she must also do it legally.

Finally, if the church is to respond to the abortion crisis in a Christlike manner, she must learn to "bear the burdens of others."[4] Galatians 6 speaks of each person bearing his own burden (Gal. 6:5) and of each person bearing the burdens of one another (Gal. 6:2). There is no contradiction. Galatians 6:2 admonishes Christians to bear the "troublesome moral faults which afflict" one another, that is, to help someone walk under the load of their wrong choices, of their tendency toward sin and their weaknesses. It means that we are to rescue those who are in error by helping them carry the burden of their weaknesses. There is no sense in which this is equivalent with accommodating evil or sin. This is not making excuses for someone's failure or rebellion, but it is equipping and preparing them for victorious living by receiving them, loving them, and helping them out of their sin. This is the challenge to the church for those who are both seeking and providing abortions.

When Michael Bray and I debated the issues in this book, he wondered aloud why the Scriptures did not comment on what Christ would have done had He come upon the man helped by the Good Samaritan while he was being beaten on the Jericho Road. He mused that perhaps those who oppose his ideas of force and violence would have stood by and said, "When you are through, we'll help the victim." He expressed the certainty that Jesus would have stepped up with a two-by-four and beaten the assailants.

As I thought and prayed during Michael's statement, it occurred to me that that is not what Jesus would have done. It is always dangerous to speculate where Scripture is silent. Yet, Michael's question fundamentally addresses the nature of Christ's incarnation and mission. It became obvious to me how, I believe, Jesus would have responded.

What Jesus would have done provides instruction for every believer in this world. What Jesus would have done provides an example for confronting evil of any kind. What Jesus would have done enables us to apply truth consistently to a situation as complex and as critical as abortion-on-demand in America.

If Jesus Christ had come upon the man on the road to Jericho as he was being beaten, I do not believe He would have picked up a weapon and attacked the assailants. He would have walked into their midst and said, "Beat Me!"

NOTES

Preface

1. Paul Pinkham, Associated Baptist Press, 2 March 1995, 1.

Chapter 1 • Violence That Demands a Response

1. Refer. to Bray occur throughout this book. The publication of his book, *A Time to Kill*, makes him one of the chief spokesmen for the pro-violence anti-abortion movement.
2. Published by Bray, originally published as *Actors in the Kingdom not Clappers in the Audience (1990, 1993)*.
3. Published by Advocates for Life Publications, Portland, Oreg., September 1994.
4. Church Rebukes Priest Who Wants Abortionists Dead," *Beaumont Enterprise*, 18 August 1993.
5. *Life Advocate Magazine* (Portland, Oreg.; n.d., n.p.p.).
6. Personal correspondence circulated by Trosch.
7. In a 23 August 1993 telephone conversation, Trosch proposed that the personages at the Transfiguration was a tacit approval by God of "violent zeal." This question will be dealt with later in this volume.
8. Letter from Trosch, 20 June 1994, circulated to many, asking them to answer the same questions.
9. Tamar Lewin, "Abortion Providers Attempt to Handle Growing Threat," *New York Times*, 31 December 1994.
10. Catherine S. Manegold, "Anti-Abortion Groups Disavow New Killings," *New York Times*, 1 January 1995.
11. Jill Smolowe, "Fear in the Land," *Time*, 8 January 1995.
12. The National Right to Life Committee, quoted in the *Washington Post*, 30 July 1994.

13. Anthony Lewis, "The Absolute Truth," *New York Times*, 1 August 1994.
14. James L. Holly, "Blame versus Balance," *Beaumont Enterprise*, 21 March 1993.
15. "Clinic Killings," *Washington Post*, 2 August 1994.
16. Paul Greenberg, "Massacre Outside Clinic Shows Need for Vigilance," *Beaumont Enterprise*, 7 August 1994.
17. The Christian Life Commission of the Southern Baptist Convention's twelve-page statement is entitled, "The Struggle Against Abortion: Why the Use of Lethal Force Is Not Morally Justifiable."
18. Michael Bray, *A Time to Kill* (Portland, Oreg.: Advocates for Life Publications, n.d.), 173ff.
19. Back cover, ibid.
20. Face to Face with Life, Death—Academic Article by Gunman's Lawyer OK'd Anti-abortion Killing before Fatal Shooting," *Beaumont Enterprise*, 28 August 1994. Michael Hirsh was identified as the author of the law review article. Hirsh was representing Paul Hill on an unrelated charge involving his right to free speech in "harassing abortion clinic workers." After Hill's shooting of Britton and Barrett, Hirsh asked that the law review article be withdrawn because "he was very concerned about the potential it could have on his career . . . particularly if there were further shootings of abortion doctors."
21. Unpublished manuscript, 36, 90, 91.

Chapter 2 • Sanctity of Human Life

1. See Bill McBean, "The Elderly Terminally Ill 'Have a Duty to Die,' Lamm Says," *Rocky Mountain News*, 28 March 1984.
   Then Governor Richard Lamm has continued to press for "voluntary euthanasia" as director of the Center for Public Policy and Contemporary Issues at the University of Denver. ("Abortion Foes Say Romer Panel Backs Euthanasia," *Rocky Mountain News*, 6 April 1991.) Lamm has endorsed the Hemlock Society's publication, *Final Exit: The Practicalities of Self-Deliverance and Assisted Suicide for the Dying*, by Derek Humphry (Linda Castrone, "Last Wish Book Advises Terminally Ill on Euthanasia," *Rocky Mountain News*, 22 August 1991).
2. See Jack Kevorkian's *Prescription Medicide* (New York: Prometheus Books, 1991). "Kevorkian recommends making

euthanasia a medical subspecialty, with doctors who specialize in following terminal patients through death."

3. Nora Zamichow, "Newsletter Articles Stir Furor in High-IQ Group Opinion," *Los Angeles Times,* 10 January 1995.

4. One of the principle arguments against pornography is found here. At its foundation, pornography is rooted in the proposition that one person can use another person for profit without regard to the welfare of the person being used. On the basis of the providence of God, Scripture rejects that idea. When one accepts responsibility for another person in any social transaction, exploitation, such as in pornography, is excluded from Christian conduct.

5. Charles Hodge, *Systematic Theology* (Reprint ed., Grand Rapids, Mich.: Eerdmans, 1981), 2:96ff.

6. For more on this see "The Life of Samson: Strengthened Through Submission: Sanctioned Through Sacrifice," in *Men's Conference Manual,* vol. 1, published by Mission and Ministry to Men, Inc.

7. The Nazarite vow is described in Num. 6:1-21. The Nazarite was required not to cut his hair, not to drink wine and not to touch a dead body. Each of these has spiritual applications in the life of Christians.

8. Ps. 139:14-16.

Chapter 3 • Operation Rescue

1. For a detailed discussion of this issue see *Covetousness, Contentment and Complacency,* published by Mission and Ministry to Men, Inc.

Chapter 4 • The Roots of Violence

1. A review of Randall Terry's life is found in Mary T. Schimich, "An Explosive Issue's Leading Crusaders; Strategies Are Being Remapped As the Action Moves Back to the States," *Chicago Tribune,* 24 July 1989.

2. Randall Terry, *Operation Rescue* (Springdale, Pa.: Whitaker House, 1989), 18.

3. See "Operation Rescue to Target Judges, DAS in New Tactic," *Atlanta Constitution,* 13 April 1990.

4. Terry, *Operation Rescue,* 19.

5. Ibid., 20.

6. Ibid., 24.

7. "Operation Rescue: The Civil-Rights Movement of the Nineties," *Policy Review,* no. 47 (Winter 1989): 82-83.

8. "Anti-abortion Group Seeking to Create 'Social Tension,'" *Miami Herald,* 3 January 1989.

9. Terry, *Operation Rescue,* 50-52.

10. "Abortion Foes Seek New Image," *Christian Science Monitor,* 13 July 1993; "Abortion Foes Strike at Doctors' Homes/Lives Illegal Intimidation or Protected Protest?" *Washington Post,* 8 April 1993; Joe Maxwell, "Sizing Up a New Target Randall Terry Steps Down from Operation Rescue to Go on the Attack Against Bill Clinton," *Chicago Tribune,* 15 August 1994, in which Terry said, "This is a deplorable act, and Operation Rescue will maintain its unswerving adherence to non-violence . . . the anti-abortion movement has been 'desperately hurt' by the 1993 and 1994 killings. There's no question about that."

Chapter 5 • Revolution and Civil Disobedience

1. Michael Bray, *A Time to Kill* (Portland, Oreg.: Advocates for Life Publications, n.d.), 158, 161, 164.

2. Ibid., 161.

3. Ibid., 164.

4. Ibid., 151, 158, 160, 161, 169.

5. Randall Terry, *Operation Rescue* (Springdale, Pa.: Whitaker House, 1989), 110-11.

6. Bonhoeffer's friend and student Eberhard Bethge wrote his biography, *Dietrich Bonhoeffer: Man of Vision, Man of Courage,* trans. Eric Mosbacher et al. (New York: Harper & Row, 1977).

7. Kenneth Earl Morris, *Ethic of Discipleship: A Study in Social Psychology, Political Thought, and Religion* (University Park: Pennsylvania State University Press, 1986), 6.

8. Ibid., 20.

9. Bonhoeffer's pilgrimage to this point is documented in ibid.

10. Dietrich Bonhoeffer, *The Cost of Discipleship* (New York: Macmillan, 1963), 99.

11. Ibid., 208.

12. Ibid., 289-91.

13. Ibid., 291.

14. Ibid., 293, 296-297.

15. Terry argues that "two truths must be pointed out" about

American slavery. One is "American slavery and biblical slavery have virtually nothing in common," and the other is that "there is a great difference between being 'anti-slavery' and being an 'abolitionist'." See also David Brion David, *The Problem of Slavery in Western Culture* (Ithaca: Cornell University Press, 1966).

16. Francis A. Schaeffer, *A Christian Manifesto* (Wheaton, Il.: Crossway Books, 1981), 117.

17. Ibid., 46.

18. Ibid.

19. Ibid., 92, quoted in Terry, *Operation Rescue*, 101-102.

20. Terry, *Operation Rescue*, 106.

21. Michael Bray, *When Bricks Bleed I'll Cry* (n.p.p.: n.p., 1993), 49.

Chapter 6 • Obeying God or Man?

1. Michael Bray, *When Bricks Bleed I'll Cry* (n.p.p.: n.p., 1993), 15.

2. Francis A. Schaeffer, *A Christian Manifesto* (Wheaton, Il.: Crossway Books, 1981), 58.

3. Ibid., 108.

4. Ibid., 101.

5. Ibid., 124.

6. Ibid., 131.

7. Randall Terry, *Operation Rescue* (Springdale, Pa.: Whitaker House, 1989), 195.

8. Schaeffer, *Christian Manifesto*, 107, 118, 120.

9. Ibid., 128.

10. Ibid., 93.

11. Ibid., 130.

12. Ibid., 49.

Chapter 7 • Scriptures Used by the Advocates of Pro-life Violence

1. *Biblical Perspectives* 2, No. 4 (July-August 1989): 4-5.

2. *Thayer's Greek-English Lexicon of the New Testament* (Grand Rapids, Mich.: Baker Book House, 1984), 604.

3. Paul Hill, "Defensive Action," 2.

4. Ibid.

5. Michael Bray, *A Time to Kill* (Portland, Oreg.: Advocates for Life Publications, n.d.), 43.

6. The Luke 22 passage is a difficult passage to interpret independent of the rest of the Scripture. What is clear is that it does not justify

the use of shotguns to bring righteousness to the earth. Two studies that give balance and insight into this passage are I. Howard Marshall, *The Gospel of Luke*, The New International Greek Testament Commentary (Grand Rapids, Mich.: Eerdmans, 1978), and Joseph A. Fitzmyer, *The Gospel According to Luke (X-XXIV)*, The Anchor Bible (Garden City, NY: Doubleday & Co., 1985).

7. Michael Bray, *When Bricks Bleed I'll Cry* (n.p.p.: n.p., 1993), 103.

Chapter 8 • Rejecting Violence

1. For more on this see, *Judge Not That Ye Be Not Judged: A Study in Biblical Accountability*, published by Mission and Ministry to Men, Inc.

2. *Sermons of Martin Luther* (Grand Rapids, Mich.: Baker Book House, 1983), 3:119.

3. Ibid., 7:53ff.

4. Ibid., 7:56ff.

5. Michael Bray, *When Bricks Bleed I'll Cry* (n.p.p.: n.p., 1993), 103.

6. Ibid., 104

7. Blaine Harden, "Karadzik Key to Peace in Bosnia," *Washington Post*, 10 November 1992; Jonathan Landay, "Serb 'Cleansing' of Eastern Bosnia Nearly Complete," *Christian Science Monitor*, 19 March 1993.

8. Bray, *When Bricks Bleed*, 186, 187, 188, 189.

Chapter 9 • Is Abortion a New Holocaust?

1. Michael Bray, *When Bricks Bleed I'll Cry* (n.p.p.: n.p., 1993), 61.

2. Ibid., 61.

3. Nicholas de Lange, "The Impact of the Holocaust," *Atlas of the Jewish World* (New York: Facts on File, 1992), 126.

4. Judith Miller, *One by One by One* (New York: Touchstone, 1990), 9, 281-82, 287.

5. A different assessment of the use of the term *holocaust* is given in James T. Burtchaell, *Rachel Weeping: The Case Against Abortion* (New York: Harper & Row, 1984). This is a worthwhile contrast with the argument given herein.

6. Joseph E. Persico, *Nuremberg: Infamy on Trial* (New York: Penguin Books, 1994) gives excellent documentation of the position taken here.

7. Michael Hirsh to James L. Holly, 8 September 1994.

8. Michael Hirsh, "Use of Force in Defense of Another: An Argument for Michael Griffin," 40.
9. Ibid., 45.
10. Ibid., 46.
11. Ibid., 48.
12. Recall from chapter 1 Trosch's statement in which he said that the actions of Michael Griffin prepared the way for an "international holocaust" ("Church Rebukes Priest Who Wants Abortionists Dead," *Beaumont Enterprise,* 18 August 1993).
13. Bray, *When Bricks Bleed,* 61.
14. Hirsh, "Use of Force," 76.
15. Ibid.
16. Ibid., 77.

Chapter 10 • Society and Success or Faithfulness v. Effectiveness

1. Michael Hirsh, "Use of Force in Defense of Another: An Argument for Michael Griffin," 188.
2. Ibid., 178.
3. Ibid., 173.
4. Ibid., 56ff.
5. Ibid., 24ff.
6. Michael Bray, *A Time to Kill* (Portland, Oreg.: Advocates for Life Publications, n.d.), 17.
7. For a heartbreaking look into why women seek abortions, see Frederica Mathewes-Green, "Why Women Choose Abortion," *Christianity Today,* January 1995.
8. Bray, *A Time to Kill,* 18.

Chapter 11 • Advocates of Violence

1. Marlon Manuel, "True Believer Came to Hate Abortion, Bless Violence," *Atlanta Constitution,* 2 October 1994.
2. Paul Hill, "Defensive Action," 1-2.
3. Ibid., 2.
4. For more on this see, *The Hand That Struck the Face of Jesus,* published by Mission and Ministry to Men, Inc.
5. On October 7-8, 1994, this writer debated Michael Bray at Covenant Baptist Church in Columbia, Maryland, on the proposition "Is the Killing of Abortion Providers Just?" This statement was made in a personal conversation at the debate.

6. Sandy Banisky, "Bowie Family Condones Anti-abortion Violence," *Baltimore Sun,* 9 October 1994.

7. Steve Brunsman, "A Voice of Restraint: Holly Challenges Fellow Anti-abortionists Who Preach Violence," *Houston Post,* 20 November 1994.

8. Michael Bray, *A Time to Kill* (Portland, Oreg.: Advocates for Life Publications, n.d.), 34.

9. Ibid., 31-32.

10. Ibid.

11. Ibid., 42-43.

12. Ibid., 44.

13. For the distinction between loving those who hate us and helping those who hate God, see *Helping Those Who Hate the Lord: A Study of II Chronicles 19:2,* published by Mission and Ministry to Men, Inc.

14. Bray, *A Time to Kill,* 71.

15. Reinhold Niebuhr, *The Children of Light and the Children of Darkness: A Vindication of Democracy and a Critique of Its Traditional Defense* (New York, Scribner's, 1972), xi.

16. Ibid., 85. (Shelly Shannon shot Dr. Tiller in Witchita.)

17. David Trosch to James L. Holly.

18. David Trosch to Cardinal Ratzinger, circulated by Trosch, 3 of 8.

19. David Trosch to Jean A. Elmore, executive director, Media Associates Resource Coalition, Inc., 25 July 1994, 4.

20. Ibid., 4 of 4.

Chapter 12 • Who Can Use Force?

1. Michael Bray, *A Time to Kill* (Portland, Oreg.: Advocates for Life Publications, n.d.), 58.

2. For more on this concept, see, "The Seven Characteristics of the Spirit-filled Life," in *Walking and Living Habitually in the Holy Spirit, Men's Manual,* vol. 2, published by Mission and Ministry to Men, Inc.

3. Michael Bray, *When Bricks Bleed I'll Cry* (n.p.p.: n.p., 1993), 33. Second Thessalonians 2:6-7 speaks of the "Restrainer of evil," but no one imagines that that restrainer is the threat of violence by Christians.

4. Bray, *When Bricks Bleed,* 24-25.

5. Bray, *A Time to Kill,* 26-27.

6. B. F. Westcott and F. J. A. Hort, *Introduction to the New*

Testament in the Original Greek with Notes on Selected Readings (Peabody, Mass.: Hendrickson Publishers, 1988), app. 1: "Notes on Selected Readings," 87.

Chapter 13 • Go to the Spring of the Waters!

1. It is important for believers to know that today miscarriages and barrenness do not necessarily have the same implications of the judgment of God that they had in Israel.
2. Bolton Davidheiser, *Evolution and the Christian Faith* (n.p.: Presbyterian and Reformed Press, 1965).
3. Norma McCorvey and Andy Meisler, *I Am Roe* (n.p.: Harper Collins, 1994), reported in "A Tough Roe to Hoe: Abortion-rights Protagonist Shares Her Story," *Houston Chronicle,* 5 July 1994.
4. Richard Vara, "Professor Says Evolution Lacks Scientific Evidence," *Houston Chronicle,* 22 June 1991.
5. Tom Bethell was editor of *The Washington Monthly.*
6. *Harper's Magazine* (February 1976), reprinted in *Christianity Today,* 17 June 1977, 12ff.
7. Quoted from *Harper's Magazine* (February 1985): 61; D. A Carson and John D. Woodbridge, eds., *Hermeneutics, Authority, and Canon* (Grand Rapids, Mich.: Zondervan, 1986), 269.
8. A. E. Wilder Smith, *The Natural Sciences Know Nothing of Evolution* (n.p.p.: Master Books, 1981), 4.
9. L. Russ Bush and Tom J. Nettles, *Baptists and the Bible* (n.p.p.: Moody Press, 1980), 337ff.

Chapter 14 • A Modest Proposal

1. When Jesus entered Simon the Pharisee's house in Luke 7, He apparently did not immediately begin to tell him all the things that were wrong with his life. Jesus expected that the quality of His life would influence Simon. There is a balance between preaching the truth and thereby telling people where their lives are wrong (2 Tim. 4:2-3) and being involved in their lives long enough to earn the right to speak to them about their life.
2. For more on this, see, *Elijah: Clarifying the Choice, I Kings 18:17-40,* published by Mission and Ministry to Men, Inc.
3. Randolph C. Byrd, M.D., *The Southern Medical Journal,* 81, no. 7 (July 1988): 826ff.
4. There is a righteous way to do sidewalk counseling in front of

an abortion clinic. It involves the exercise of the freedoms of speech and lawful assembly without encroaching the rights of the person or those being confronted with the evil of abortion. Many churches already have prayer ministries, some cover twenty-four hours a day, seven days a week; the prayer experiment could be plugged right into these existing schedules.

6. The imprecatory psalms certainly give a model for praying that evil will befall our enemies, but they do not require such. Those psalms suggest that evil is prayed against one's enemies primarily so the name of God is not profaned.

7. Remember that Deut. 15:7-11 established the principle of "open-handed" giving; that is, giving not according to your perception but according to the perception of the one to whom you are giving. Jesus repeated this principle in Matt. 6:22-23.
   Meeting the needs of those who are seeking abortions will not be accomplished by our giving them what we perceive they need; it will be done by giving them what they perceive they need. This distinguishes Christian giving from secular welfare programs as the latter is often preoccupied with preventing fraud and abuse, while Christian charity leaves such concerns to God.

8. For more on this see *The Basis of Victory in Spiritual Warfare: The Blood of Christ*, published by Mission and Ministry to Men, Inc.

9. The dichotomy between the religious and the righteous is the foundation of Paul's message on love in 1 Corinthians 13.
   J. B. Phillips's paraphrase of this chapter is particularly helpful.

Chapter 15 • What Will Christ Have Us Do?

1. For a more detailed examination of this issue, see *Covetousness, Contentment and Complacency*, published by Mission and Ministry to Men, Inc.

2. Many pro-life activists understand this connection. Bray goes so far as to suggest that the only effective way that racism can be rejected by the Christian church is by the advocacy and promotion of interracial marriages.

3. The blood of Christ is applied to an individual's life by the confession of sin, the repentance from sin, and the receiving of the Lord Jesus Christ as personal savior.

4. For more on this concept, see, *Bearing One Another's Burdens: Galatians 6:1-5*, published by Mission and Ministry to Men, Inc.